STANDARDS FOR LEARNING

Acknowledgments

The author thanks the following people for specific advice and contributions to this publication: Faye Brownbridge, Arlene Christie, Judith Dubé, Guy Giroux, Wayne Nicolas, Julia Popwell, and Christa Volk.

The author also gratefully acknowledges the Calgary Catholic School District for granting permission to interview educators whose work is herein described.

Standards
for
Learning

Clarifying language arts outcomes
amd helping students reach them

Graham Foster

Pembroke Publishers Limited

Dedicated to Marj and Kevin

© 1998   Pembroke Publishers Limited
        538 Hood Road
        Markham, Ontario, Canada L3R 3K9

Canadian Cataloguing in Publication Data

Foster, Graham
   Standards for learning

Includes bibliographical references and index.
ISBN 1-55138-092-7

1. Language arts (Elementary). 2. Language arts (Secondary). I. Title.

LB1576.F696 1998   407   C98-930018-8

Editor: Kate Revington
Design: John Zehethofer
Cover Photography: Ajay Photographics
Typesetting: Jay Tee Graphics Ltd.

Printed and bound in Canada on acid-free paper.
10 9 8 7 6 5 4 3 2 1

Contents

Implications of a Standards and Outcomes Emphasis in Language Arts

The Current Reality

In attempting to capture the essence of a standards and outcomes emphasis on curriculum, especially in the language arts curriculum, I am reminded of a friend's description of much educational jargon: "It's like trying to get your hands on a greased hippopotamus!" While standards, outcomes, and prescribed curriculum expectations have basked in a flurry of recent professional promotions and publications, writers differ significantly in their definitions and descriptions of outcomes programs.

Teachers are particularly motivated to explore the implications of an outcomes approach. Even though they might adopt alternative words such as "expectations" and "knowledge and skills," many recent curriculum documents are outcomes based. These include Ontario's 1997 Grades 1–8 Language curriculum, The Common Framework for English Language Arts (Western Protocol), and The Common Framework of Science Learning Outcomes (Pan Canadian Protocol). The list is growing longer. Teachers in several subject disciplines are motivated to get their hands on the outcomes hippopotamus — greased or otherwise.

The outcomes approach emerges amid challenges to public schooling. It is common knowledge that increasing numbers of families are opting for home schooling, charter schools and private schools in the belief that children's learning will benefit. Aware of parental demands for alternatives and accountability, departments of education have embraced outcomes curricula. By doing so, they hope to gauge the success of disparate instructional practices and structures — an elusive goal at the moment. With precise outcomes, it may be easier to compare the merits of competing educational approaches.

The outcomes emphasis also ties in with attacks on prevalent language arts methodologies, especially whole language. A Canadian Press article, published in the *Calgary Herald* on June 14, 1997, described the language arts curriculum just announced for Ontario as "tossing out the bureaucratic 'babble' and bringing a tough new curriculum that should make elementary students learn faster and cover more ground than kids anywhere else in Canada" — hardly a subtle political message! Note the implicit faith that the clear specification of high expectations results in improved learning.

An outcomes emphasis might initially suggest that whole language no longer has a place in the classroom. The newspaper article continues: "There's no mention of the controversial teaching method called whole language. It encourages children to write almost impulsively, without paying too much heed to spelling and grammar." With the attack against whole language international, instructional practice is greatly in flux. A November 1997 *Atlantic Monthly* article, "The Reading Wars" by Nicholas Lemann, concludes that the "traditional side is now winning the battle between traditional and progressive education."

While advocates of holistic language instruction shudder at inaccurate presentations of their instructional practice, they must recognize the pressure to relate holistic instruction to the achievement of outcomes. They must also see the necessity of communicating that relationship to students, parents and the community. This book argues that advocates of holistic language learning need not be discouraged by an outcomes approach. Holistic teachers can hold to their conviction that knowledgeable, coordinated, holistic practice is centrally related to students' achievement of expectations.

Meanwhile, increased testing has sharpened and sometimes narrowed the focus on standards. In 1993 the School Achievement Indicators Program, sponsored by all provincial ministers of education in Canada, compared the provinces and territories for the achievement of literacy standards. A more comprehensive interpretation of standards was presented by a 1996 publication of the International Reading Association and the National Council of Teachers of English, *Standards for the English Language Arts*. In analysing these initiatives, teachers note considerable variation in the definition of "standards" as well as in outcomes and assessment tasks selected for standard setting.

Language arts teachers wonder whether the effects of current attention to standards and outcomes will be regressive. Many teachers shudder at the thought of a rerun of behavioral objectives such as "Nine times out of ten, students will place a comma after introductory subordinate clauses." Will a standards and outcomes emphasis negate or support what many teachers believe to be best practice in language arts instruction? In exploring the question, language arts teachers will benefit from a review of what recent publications describe as key features of an outcomes curriculum and of language arts standards. The reality is that while professional writers and curriculum documents vary in their definitions and interpretations, the variance challenges teachers to advocate those interpretations which most effectively foster children's language learning.

Before reading the summary of features of a standards and outcomes emphasis, you might benefit from reviewing your own perspectives about them. Throughout the book, there are sections marked "Professional Development Focus" to encourage reflection by individual readers or by groups of readers. This is the first:

PROFESSIONAL DEVELOPMENT FOCUS:
Reflecting on Standards and Outcomes

• What is your personal understanding of "standards" and "outcomes"?

• How do you feel about increased emphasis on "standards" and "outcomes"? Will the emphasis benefit children's learning in language arts?

• How does a standards and outcomes approach compare to your current approach to language arts instruction?

• How has your school interpreted its language arts program and literacy-related commitments to students and parents? Could it do so more effectively?

Features of a Standards and Outcomes Emphasis

Frequently, but not unanimously, the following themes emerge in the works of writers who discuss the outcomes approach:

- a focus on what students will learn rather than what teachers will teach;
- specific language to describe expectations. ("Summarize," "recall" and "distinguish" are in; "appreciate" and "understand" are out.);
- a suggestion that in units of work, teachers clearly interpret targeted expectations to students and parents;
- an argument that schools stress life skills which students will require to survive and thrive after graduation;
- advocacy of multidisciplinary learning;
- an insistence that teachers modify programs, that they plan remediation and enrichment, as well as student options in content, learning activities, time allotments, and assessment.

These outcomes themes, or features, contain specific implications for assessment and for the establishment of assessment standards. The outcomes philosophy nudges educators toward increased emphasis on performance assessment, for which a student synthesizes knowledge and illustrates ability in an authentic task. Assessment criteria should be clearly worded and specific. Rubrics, which describe desired performance features and gradations of performance, and exemplars, which present student work of varying quality, are critically important. The use of rubrics and exemplars will help teachers, students, and parents to understand curricular expectations.

Subsequent chapters explore the impact that the six features of a standards and outcomes emphasis outlined above have on language arts instruction. Clearly, outcomes implications will differ among teachers depending on a teacher's current knowledge, beliefs, and classroom practice. Teachers who have completed recent studies in language arts probably need not feel threatened by an enlightened standards and outcomes emphasis. While they are always wise to maintain a critical stance to any curriculum innovation, they should employ the current standards and outcomes focus to consolidate, coordinate and promote the best instructional practice.

CHAPTER TWO

Features of Outcomes Programs

A Focus on Learning Rather than Teaching

Teachers in all subject disciplines are familiar with curriculum outlines. With the accent on instruction rather than on learning, these curricula specify a teacher's legal responsibility regarding instruction.

Often, past programs of study legislated, or, at least strongly implied, certain methodologies, such as a themes approach, an inquiry approach, a problem-solving approach, an activity-based approach, a process approach or the many interpretations of a "whole language" approach. Frequently professional literature advocated these approaches which were received with skepticism in the popular press!

By focusing on what students are expected to learn rather than on what teachers are expected to teach, an outcomes approach offers teachers greater leeway with methodology than earlier programs may have. With an outcomes approach the message is clear: Within reason, we don't particularly care how you help students reach the outcomes. However, your job is to bring them there. While teachers will find that outcomes curricula offer methodological leeway, the documents still imply methodology. For example, outcomes related to collaborative learning in small groups cannot be achieved through a steady diet of worksheets.

At its best, an outcomes approach recognizes that methodology is the teacher's choice. While other curriculum frameworks challenge artistic planning and instruction, the outcomes framework trumpets the familiar theme of freedom with responsibility. With an outcomes approach, teachers implement a process or an inquiry or a literature circles approach, not because they are mandated to do so, but because they know and believe that such an approach will help students achieve outcomes.

In analysing curriculum documents that have been influenced by an outcomes approach, teachers should determine whether the mandated program includes processes in the list of outcomes or whether the outcomes are skills. While all outcomes curricula will minimize teachers' methodological prescriptions, outcomes-based language arts curricula will differ in their inclusion of processes used by students.

A focus on definitions is critical. The previous paragraph mentioned "processes" and "outcomes"; earlier paragraphs have discussed "methodology." Teachers should not assume widespread consensus about the meaning of familiar jargon. In fact, confusion about "processes" and "methodology" will hamper intelligent implementation of an outcomes-based language arts program.

- **Methodology** refers to a *teacher's* instructional approaches, such as lecture, seatwork, writing workshop, small-group, conferences, and literature circles.

  Outcomes curricula do not mandate methodology.

- **Outcomes** refer to expectations for student achievement. They include skills and may include processes or strategies.

- **Skills** refer to those abilities which students are expected to demonstrate — the *what* of instruction. For example, one recently developed outcomes curriculum calls for Grade 5 students to demonstrate skills such as the following: identifying key elements and technique in oral literature and media and exploring their impact; gathering and recording information and ideas using a plan; recognizing organizational patterns of text; revising for content, organization and clarity; writing legibly and using word processing when composing and revising; and selecting words for appropriate connotations and using varied lengths and structures.

Most, but not all, of the outcomes specified in language arts curricula, at least in Canada, can be classified as skills.

- **Processes/Strategies** refer to the *know-how* of competent language users. Processes/strategies are *not* the same as methodologies since students are expected to employ them.

Typical reading processes and strategies include building background knowledge; predicting; envisioning or visualizing; questioning; summarizing; rereading for sense; chunking text (especially important in reading poetry); recalling personal experience related to text; and using graphic organizers or key visuals.

Commonly recognized writing processes and strategies include freewriting; brainstorming; using graphic organizers and key visuals; note making; reviewing writing variables (role, purpose, audience, format); dramatizing and role-playing; leaving a space when the word doesn't come; beginning to write the section that the writer finds most comfortable; reading aloud with a partner; revising with specific criteria.

Professional sources have long argued that while all students benefit from strategic instruction, low-average and below-average students require it most. Effective readers and writers frequently and intuitively use a range of strategies. Struggling readers and writers benefit from instruction in the know-how of successful readers and writers.

Regardless of the prescribed program's degree of emphasis on process or strategy, an outcomes approach underlines the reason for teachers to plan for process instruction. Much research indicates that students who have command of a wide repertoire of strategies achieve skills more successfully. An accessible source of research on the importance of reading strategies is *New Directions in Reading Instruction*, by Joy Monahan and Bess Hinson. George Hillocks' *Research on Written Composition* and his 1995 publication, *Teaching Writing as Reflective Practice*, establish the importance of processes and strategies in the development of writing skill.

Language arts teachers would be wise to draw on the current discussion about outcomes to refine their messages to students and parents about links between process and content. In recent years, teachers have sometimes been maligned for emphasizing process at the expense of content. Rather than abandoning their commitment to process instruction, teachers should use the implementation of an outcomes curriculum to stress the importance of process and strategies. They can communicate to parents that process fosters rather than replaces the development of skill and the learning of content. The current reality impels language arts teachers to proclaim their commitment to those processes which help students achieve outcomes.

PROFESSIONAL DEVELOPMENT FOCUS:
Emphasizing Process Instruction

- Review the outcomes or expectations specified for the grade(s) you teach to check for emphasis on processes and strategies. You might use a highlighter for those outcomes which can be classified as processes or strategies.

- How will you help your students meet outcomes or expectations that are processes or strategies by nature?

- An outcomes approach offers you latitude in methodology. What methodological practices seem to be most appropriate for the outcomes specified for the grade(s) that you teach?

- How will you describe to parents the language arts program which operates in your classroom?

Specific Language to Describe Outcomes

The outcomes imperative that teachers express expectations with specific verbs has a familiar ring. A generation ago, teachers considered a similar challenge in their work with Bloom's taxonomy and taxonomies such as Barrett's taxonomy for reading. At that time many teachers argued that embracing Bloom's taxonomy was a Faustian bargain: the effort to clarify expectations simplified complex language performance. They shunned the "brave new world" of those who would reduce language learning to that which can be predicted and precisely described.

Perhaps the time since the original debate over behavioral objectives has brought language arts educators to sensible middle ground. Many teachers concur that while they are wise to be as precise as possible in describing expectations, for many important language arts outcomes, less precise language cannot be avoided. Indeed, it is desirable. Many would agree with Arthur Applebee that descriptive language can never totally capture the personal and aesthetic quality of writing and literature. "At best in transactional writing we can isolate one strand of one process of constructing, analyzing and clarifying its constituent parts" (*The Child's Concept of Story*, p. 131).

Some language arts teachers may take heart when they review the mixture of precise and less-precise outcomes listed in recent curriculum documents. For instance, the Western Protocol for English language arts, developed for Manitoba, Saskatchewan, Alberta, British Columbia, Yukon Territory, and Northwest Territories, requires Grade 6 students to "edit for subject-verb agreement, appropriate verb tense and correct pronoun references." A less precise outcome is that Grade 6 students will "seek connections between previous experiences, prior knowledge and a variety of texts." Ontario's Grades 1–8 Language is also more or less precise in expectations. By the end of Grade 6, students will "produce media texts using writing and materials from other media"; they will also "use subordinate clauses correctly." However, even this last outcome is complicated in that students who "correctly" use subordinate clauses in worksheet exercises do not necessarily do so in their writing.

Language arts teachers have long debated the desirable level of specificity in a language arts curriculum document. No matter what their position on this question, though, most teachers will agree that students should apply skills in context, an emphasis that is stronger than that of the behavioral objectives era. An outcomes curriculum should not imply a regression to the good old days of decontextualized subskill teaching guided by a workbook. Quite the opposite!

There is a critical difference between the recent outcomes-inspired language arts curricula and many of their predecessors: the specificity of grammar and usage outcomes. For instance, in Alberta's 1987 Junior High language arts curriculum, grammar and usage received one mention amid about 190 other skills specified for each of Grades 7, 8, and 9: "The student will be able to edit, with some assistance, for correctness of expression, especially proofreading for errors in sentence structure, punctuation, capitalization, grammar, usage and spelling." The much more recent Western Protocol, on the other hand, specifies that Grade 7 students are expected to edit for consistent verb tense, to know and apply spelling conventions to unfamiliar words, and to know and adopt capitalization and punctuation conventions in simple, compound and complex sentences when editing and proofreading. The parallel Ontario document is even more prescriptive. For example, for Grade 7, it lists four expectations under the heading "Grammar," two under "Punctuation," and three under "Spelling." The trend is readily apparent.

What are the practical consequences for the language arts teacher?

Specificity about grammar and usage outcomes challenges language arts teachers to review their beliefs about direct instruction. While few would argue that consistent verb tense is usually (not always) a desirable feature in Grade 7 writing, the $64,000 question is: How do teachers encourage Grade 7 students to meet the outcome of consistent verb tense in their writing?

I would argue that language arts teachers should remember years of research about the importance of the contextual development of skills — that students apply the skill in their own writing. The point is clearly established in George Hillocks' summary of research into writing, *Research on Written Composition*, and Constance Weaver's summary of research into instruction in grammar, *Grammar for Teachers, Perspectives and Definitions*, and the more recent *Teaching Grammar in Context* (1996). A useful reference for contextual instruction in spelling and grammar in the elementary grades is Australian Lesley Wing Jan's *Spelling and Grammar in a Whole Language Classroom*.

The following practical advice offers one approach for contextual instruction in grammar usage.

1. For writing completed early in the school year, focus student revision on aspects of form, content, organization and structure which are appropriate for students' purpose and audience. Ask students to revise using specific criteria related to content, organization and form. Do not emphasize usage in early writing assignments.

2. From students' writing (*not* subskill tests), assess whether usage outcomes are being met.

3. If students are not meeting a usage outcome, plan a mini-lesson for the class or a group of students. Although reference books and exercises may be helpful, students should always

apply their learning of language conventions to their own writing. For example, if a Grade 7 student found examples of inconsistent verb tense in her writing, she should make the editing changes there.

4. Ensure that students have access to dictionaries, handbooks and spelling references and encourage them to use these references independently. Students may need to work on outcomes specified for another grade because their writing indicates the need. Obviously, independent work may be pursued in matters of content, organization, syntax, and vocabulary, as well as usage. Independent work should be dated and kept, possibly in a special section of a notebook or in a file.

5. Encourage students to employ revision and editing criteria related to their personal writing goals as well as to the particular composition. These criteria should be specific. For example: "Check for consistent verb tense" is preferable to the general "Check for correct grammar." Again, students should engage in revision with specific criteria related to content, organization, sentence structure, and vocabulary. Editing for correctness is not enough.

6. If individual students are still struggling to demonstrate an expectation in their writing, you may suggest further independent study or group work, as well as further revision and editing work with a related specific criterion.

7. Coordinate the following key program features with colleagues in your school:
   • encouraging students to write frequently and sometimes with choice of content and form;
   • emphasizing matters of form, content, organization and sentence structure in writing completed early in the term;
   • incorporating diagnostic direct instruction which includes, but does not exaggerate the importance of, language conventions;
   • encouraging students' goal setting and independent work with writing references;

- encouraging student work with specific criteria to revise and edit their writing. (Some of these specific criteria should relate to each student's personal writing goals.)

Skills Instruction in a Language Arts Program, which I co-authored with Judy MacKay and Claudette Miller, presents a model for teaching skills in context. The seven pieces of advice are consistent with the following model:

TEACHING SKILLS IN CONTEXT

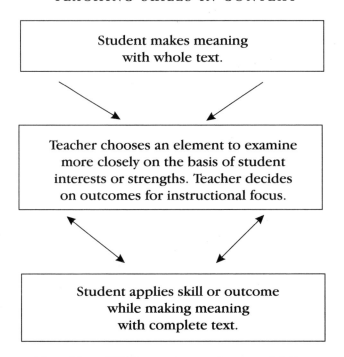

— Adapted from *Skills Instruction in a Language Arts Program*

Language arts teachers are wise to explain their instructional approach to specific skills — an approach which includes timely direct instruction and which extends beyond punctuation, grammar and spelling. Parents may benefit from the reminder that effective writing is characterized by much more than an absence of error.

Communication of Expectations to Students and Parents

"Letting students in on the secrets" and "de-mystifying" curriculum for students and parents are familiar themes in teachers' professional literature. An outcomes approach to curriculum chimes in and amplifies these themes. Few teachers would argue against the notion that students must not be left to guess about expectations. Most teachers would agree that providing parents and students with oral and written specification of instructional focus in a unit is desirable.

In an attempt to foster communication of expectations, outcomes-based curricula prescribe different outcomes for every grade or level. Many language arts teachers will find that the result is hair-splitting. For example, one recently prescribed outcomes-based language arts curriculum calls for Grade 5 students to "revise and edit their work, seeking feedback from others on content, organization and appropriateness of vocabulary for audience." Grade 6 students are expected to "revise and edit their work in collaboration with others, seeking and evaluating feedback and focussing on content, organization and appropriateness of vocabulary for audiences." Another outcomes-based language arts program prescribes that Grade 8 students will "formulate relevant main and subordinate questions on a topic to establish a purpose for gathering information," and Grade 9 students will "develop focused questions to establish a purpose for reading, listening and viewing information sources." Obviously, language arts expectations do not always divide clearly into grades.

Outcomes statements are also limited in helping students achieve excellence — they can never capture degrees of achievement. Grade 5 students who revise and edit their work with feedback from peers about content and organization will do so with varying degrees of competence. So will the Grade 8 students who are formulating main and subordinate questions on a topic to establish a purpose for gathering information.

Outcomes statements will not bear the burden of communication on their own. When language arts teachers try to communicate expectations to students and parents, they should recognize that, while curriculum prescriptions are helpful, they are not enough, especially when the outcomes are similar from grade to grade. For teachers to succeed in interpreting expectations, they must be sure to outline specifically other critical elements in a program:

- Resources — textual, media, and human. What resources are students expected to use in meeting the outcome? Remember that most students will find articulating themes for *Hamlet* more challenging than articulating themes for a TV show like *Baywatch*.

- Exemplars — samples of work, including print and audiovisual, which demonstrate degrees of excellence in achievement. You are wise to collect samples over several years, and to use these samples to establish expectations with colleagues.

- Context — information about the conditions under which the achievement is expected. How much time will students have? How much assistance will they receive? When are they expected to complete the work?

- Assessment Procedures — information about how achievement of the expectations will be evaluated.

Clearly, to articulate expectations effectively, language arts teachers must make their presentations to students and parents as comprehensive as possible. Resources such as the *Standards Consensus Series*, published by the National Council of Teachers of English (1997), and the *Classroom Assessment Materials Program*, published by Alberta Education (1997), are valuable assets for teachers to interpret expectations. Both of these feature student work of varying quality, assess the work according to curriculum expectations, and offer specific commentary. Future publications of this sort are critically important.

While outcomes curricula do not typically specify methodology, teachers should interpret process "know-how" to students and parents. "This is what's expected. Let me show you a good way to get there. Here's something that works for me." When modeling, the teacher thinks out loud with work in progress. More powerful than *telling* students to revise for content and to formulate questions on a topic, *showing* students how a teacher completes the task helps students discover strategies which work for them.

Finally, in interpreting language arts programs to parents, teachers should offer clear explanations. Avoid jargon, if possible, and be sure to define any jargon that you feel obliged to use. Whenever possible, show rather than tell. Always offer elaboration and examples; always avoid general labels. For instance, instead of telling parents that children will engage in a "literature circles" approach, describe features of the approach: Tell them that students will read frequently and select their own books; meet regularly to discuss their reading; follow understood procedures in their discussions of books; identify discussion topics for their literature circles; and assess their own work in literature circles to complement your observational assessment. If you have a videotape of literature circles in action, possibly from a previous year, all the better. Indicate to parents the specific outcomes that are promoted through the approach. These might include presentation of personal viewpoints; comparison of viewpoints; engagement in frequent reading; ability to recognize and assess an author's technique; ability to determine literal and implied meaning of text.

In your presentation, emphasize what parents can do to promote their children's learning and, of course, be sure to entertain parents' questions.

A particularly impressive publication in interpreting language arts programs to parents in Janie Hydrik's *Parent's Guide to Literacy for the 21st Century*. Although the book focuses on Kindergarten to Grade 5, it is a model of jargon-free program interpretation with specific invitations and suggestions for parents to cooperate in the development of children's literacy.

A Life Skills Emphasis

An outcomes focus reminds educators that school graduates must live in a rapidly changing world and that they need a flexible repertoire of abilities. While connecting school-life to the "after-life" can be trivialized to mean that students use the computer to write additional business letters and do other utilitarian tasks, the life skills emphasis need not be trivial. A review of some recent language arts outcomes curricula offers a measure of reassurance.

Many outcomes curricula identify the management of information as a major theme. Students are challenged to complete independent research, to analyse and to create media texts, to analyse and evaluate information from many sources, and to use technology to communicate. Furthermore, many curricula do not overlook speaking and listening outcomes. Those who believe that high school graduates require the ability to think critically and to demonstrate collaborative problem-solving strategies will note that these outcomes have also been emphasized consistently in outcomes curricula. Applying rather than recalling information is a major theme across the curriculum — an appropriate emphasis in future-directed education.

Language arts teachers may fear that the exuberance of an outcomes program over practical, utilitarian, transactional language may threaten personal artistic, poetic language. They understand that reading a newspaper demands a different process from that required to read a poem. They argue that education should be for the soul as well as for the career ladder.

Some curricula recognize the personal benefits of education. Such curricula emphasize that graduates' lives are enriched through the enjoyment and response to literary and media texts; by using language to explore, to learn about oneself and to define one's personhood; and through playful and artistic expression in language. Outcomes curricula can certainly be written to value the personal and the poetic as well as the practical.

In analysing new language arts curricula, teachers will want to gauge the program's personal and recreational emphasis. Many questions could be asked. To what extent does the program foster self-selected reading and response? To what extent does it encourage students to personalize literature by writing and talking about making connections to personal experience? To what extent does it encourage exploratory writing and writing about personally significant topics? To what extent does it encourage students to translate literary text into media text and to create original media texts? How well does it nudge students to note personally significant details in their lives and in text, to reflect and to question? How well does it encourage students to discover their voices as authors? All of these inquiries reflect James Britton's words: "An education limited to activity in the participant role is in the last analysis an attempt to produce men and women with the efficiency of machines" (*Language and Learning*, p. 152). Clearly, an enlightened lifestyles emphasis includes personal and aesthetic goals.

At its best, the outcomes emphasis in language arts curriculum supports another familiar theme in professional literature — communication for genuine purposes and audiences. The teacher-as-evaluator ought not to be the sole audience for students' language. Audiences should include the private audience of the self, the peer group, interested community members and public audiences.

The following examples are but a few possibilities for genuine language use:

- Students write letters to request action or response from a person who is likely to respond.

- Older students interview younger students to explore their interests; following the interviews, older students prepare stories or visual presentations for younger students.

- Students enjoy a variety of publishing opportunities — newsletters, anthologies and school displays.

- Students present oral interpretations, debates, dramatic interpretations and varied audiovisual presentations to audiences in and beyond their classroom.

- Students complete oral history projects focused on family and community members.

- Students employ community and Internet resources to answer research questions and to complete a research project.

- Students work on the Internet to communicate, to collaborate and to share publications.

Whenever possible, students should engage in self-assessment and in supportive peer-assessment of language performance. School presentations or performances provide one occasion. Invite all members of the audience to assess the presentation and to offer praise and constructive suggestions. Such practice underlines the importance of oneself and one's peers as important audiences.

PROFESSIONAL DEVELOPMENT FOCUS:
Promoting Life Skills

- Review the outcomes or expectations specified for the grade(s) that you teach. Mark outcomes or expectations which have a life skills emphasis: possibly a check for those with a practical outcomes emphasis and a star for those with a personal development emphasis. Are the personal and practical expectations balanced?

- How will you help your students meet life skills outcomes? Consider possibilities for authentic language experiences.

- How is your school promoting students' reading, writing, oral language and visual communication at home and in the community?

- How is your school promoting students' language use for varied purposes and audiences?

Multidisciplinary Learning

In reviewing outcomes-inspired language arts curricula, teachers will immediately notice that many of the outcomes apply to other disciplines. After all, reading, writing, oral language, and visual communication occur throughout the curriculum. For years, language arts teachers, especially those at the elementary level, have seized the opportunity to plan for multidisciplinary learning: learning in which language arts expectations are nurtured in science, social studies, mathematics and other subjects. While multidisciplinary attention to language expectations makes sense, it is not without pitfalls — and may be yet another Faustian bargain.

At least two arguments support the multidisciplinary approach. One is the pedagogical importance of developing skills in context, and the other is the necessity of a multidisciplinary approach in an increasingly crowded curriculum.

Still, when language arts teachers embrace a multidisciplinary approach, they must face the question What is the essence of language arts? If reading, writing, oral language, and visual communication can be taught in science, social studies and mathematics, is language arts viable as a discipline? And if that is in question, will it be crowded out of a crowded curriculum?

First, let's review the arguments in favor of a multidisciplinary approach.

One powerful argument relates to the pedagogical importance of developing skills in context. To most language arts teachers, helping students apply strategies to make sense of reading, writing and oral language in all disciplines in common sense. The authors of *Becoming a Nation of Readers* eloquently express that point. Richard Anderson and others write: "The most logical place for instruction in most reading and thinking strategies is in science and social studies rather than in separate lessons about reading. The reason is that the strategies are useful mainly when the student is grappling with unfamiliar content. Outlining and summarizing, for instance, make sense only when there is some substantial material to be outlined and summarized." (p. 73)

The Calgary Catholic School District in which I work has embarked on several language-across-the-curriculum projects. For instance, since the position paper is critically important for writing in social studies, most of the District's social studies teachers teach in context those writing process and revision strategies which are relevant to position papers. Language arts teachers attend to other discourse forms. The Calgary Catholic School District has published curriculum resources in science, social studies, and mathematics as well as language arts to encourage student use of specific revision criteria in the context of actual writing in these disciplines. Other districts have embarked on similar projects.

The second argument in favor of a multidisciplinary approach resonates with teachers dealing with a crowded curriculum. Schools are expected to handle ever-increasing content. Therefore, it makes sense to attend to language expectations throughout the curriculum whenever possible. Sometimes, teachers attend to language expectations in other subjects rather than in language arts. In other cases, teachers encourage transfer of skills and strategies as they connect the content of several disciplines. Since many students will not automatically transfer skills and strategies or make connections, teachers must often help them directly to transfer skills and strategies and to connect content.

Does language-across-the-curriculum imperil language arts in a crowded curriculum? Teachers have reason to be vigilant that it does not — especially since outcomes curricula emphasize practical utilitarian learning with a life skills emphasis. Although poetry and fiction will not pay most people's bills, surely students' lives are enriched when they interpret and compose poetry and fiction. All students are entitled to read works strong in voice and are entitled to authorized curricula that help them refine their own voices as writers.

Language arts teachers should review all curriculum revisions to ensure that literature is not simply reduced to transactional reading. Without doubt literature and literary text distinguish language arts from other disciplines. As a school subject, language arts without literature is probably doomed.

As teachers analyse any revised language arts curriculum, they should look for reassurance that students' work with literary and media text extends beyond analysis. It should include reflective writing and discussion, commentary, questioning, predicting, expressing doubts, making observations, and developing understandings. Language arts curricula should continue to encourage students to identify and describe texts which involve them and are personally meaningful. Teachers know that instruction in literary form and technique is most effective in this personal context. Without doubt, language arts teachers should review outcomes-inspired curriculum documents to ensure that literature and personal knowledge are honored.

Even if prescribed curriculum documents ignore or minimize outcomes related to independent thinking and personal knowing, teachers wisely emphasize these program features. The professional research sources that support attention to process outcomes also support attention to metacognition and reflection by students. Research reviewed by Joy Monahan and George Hillocks, cited earlier in this book, argues that reflective, strategic, and thoughtful students meet outcomes, especially performance outcomes, more efficiently than passive students. It is not insignificant that the title of George Hillocks' most recent book is *Teaching Writing as Reflective Practice*.

PROFESSIONAL DEVELOPMENT FOCUS:
Upholding the Value of Literature

- Consider language arts outcomes and expectations which can be developed and transferred to other subject disciplines.

- Review the outcomes or expectations for the grade(s) that you teach. Are student composition and interpretation of literature emphasized? Is student interaction with text adequately valued?

Planning and Program Modification

Program modification is yet another curriculum theme, sounded in professional literature for years, emphasized by outcomes literature. It is a truism that successful teachers know as much about their students as they do about curricular expectations and that the art of teaching centres on connecting the two.

While an outcomes approach itemizes expectations for a grade or level, it implies a diagnostic approach. Clearly, presenting students with impossible expectations or with expectations they have already met is unacceptable. Setting reasonable expectations so that students progress is more responsible. A clear danger of a

31

grade-specific outcomes curriculum is that it could be interpreted as a monolithic prescription for all students in the class.

What are the practical implications for the teacher?

A diagnostic approach to an outcomes-inspired language arts program has implications for planning, communication and also, methodology. Obviously, teachers will incorporate prescribed outcomes in their planning. As a sensible guideline, teachers should have a specific short-range plan for current work-in-progress with each class. Considering the importance of diagnostic instruction and program modification, teachers should not jump ahead in making several short-range plans at the beginning of the school year. While the following elements are hardly new in language arts units, an outcomes perspective stresses that assessment should be clearly linked to the outcomes or expectations highlighted in the unit.

Elements in a short-range lesson plan from an outcomes perspective

Theme or Topic: Outcomes curricula do not specify genre, theme or skill. They challenge teachers to choose themes or topics that will appeal to students in the class.

Timelines: Beginning teachers will find it sensible advice to develop short units with carefully selected expectations. Since outcomes curricula do not specify timelines for units or short-range plans, teachers are challenged to target appropriate timelines.

Outcomes or Expectations: An outcomes-based short-range plan answers the question "What should learners be able to do by the conclusion of the unit of work?" with specifics. As they plan units of work, teachers should select items from the prescribed outcomes. They should highlight those items which are critical in the unit, recognizing that countless other curriculum outcomes will receive incidental attention; these need not be included in the plan. The most effective units highlight expectations that are appropriate to the needs and interests of students in the class.

Resources: An outcomes approach extends traditional conceptions of print resources to include media, technological, and human resources. The short-range plan should answer the question "What resources will students use to meet the expectations highlighted in the unit?" The most effective language arts units identify resources which suit both the outcomes as well as the needs and interests of students in the class.

Instructional Procedures: An outcomes-based short-range plan should indicate which learning activities will be emphasized to help students meet the expectations highlighted in the unit. Activities include audiotaping, brainstorming, choral reading, oral interpretation, paired reading, reader's theatre, storyboarding, journal writing, small-group work, modeling of processes, peer tutoring, portfolio work, visual representations, semantic mapping, field trips and learning logs. For all of their school performances, students should engage in self-assessment and peer-assessment with specific, relevant criteria. Once again, effective language arts units specify instructional procedures directly related to outcomes appropriate to students in the class.

Despite its reluctance to specify methodology, a diagnostic outcomes-based curriculum demands that teachers be comfortable with varied grouping options for students. These include the following: full-class instruction; independent learning activities including those students have chosen themselves; small-group learning, such as collaborative work and peer tutoring; conferences between the teacher and individual students; instructional support offered by instructional assistants, volunteers and parents.

A range of needs and interests cannot be accommodated by a steady diet of full-class instruction. Obviously, teachers emphasize grouping options according to highlighted expectations or outcomes for their students and according to program modifications which have been identified for individual students.

Program Modification Notes: Short-range plans should briefly note program modifications for students in the class. Program modifications include different topic or timelines, different outcomes, different resources, different instructional procedures and different assessment.

Long-established wisdom in language arts suggests that most students can achieve any selected outcome if print and human resources are modified. For instance, a student who is struggling to complete a character sketch for stories in the grade level anthology will often succeed with a story that is either self-selected or less challenging.

If students are completing independent enrichment units, they should negotiate topics, timelines, outcomes, resources, instructional procedures and assessment procedures with the teacher. It is wise policy to file written copies of these individual plans or contracts.

As stressed throughout this book, an outcomes approach to language arts planning challenges teachers to communicate expectations to students and parents. This communication encourages students to take responsibility for their learning; it encourages parents to support and extend their children's learning. Schools should inform parents when their child's program has been modified in some important way, whether it be changed expectations, timelines, resources, instructional procedures, supplementary support, or assessment.

Furthermore, parents should always know when their children are following a significantly different program than that specified for the grade. Many authorities require schools to involve parents in the planning of Individual Program Plans (IPPs) for exceptional students and to have parents sign these plans.

Assessment: An outcomes-based short-range plan should specify how teachers will determine how successfully students have met the unit's highlighted expectations. Teachers must ask themselves "How will I know that students have met the central outcomes in the unit?" Ideally, assessment is wide-ranging throughout the year, related to the span of outcomes itemized for the grade. It should include the following:

- informal, observational, and anecdotal assessment;
- pre-specified response assessment, which requires students to respond to a predetermined answer;
- performance assessment, which calls for the use of criteria to judge an activity or product which cannot be predicted beforehand. Performance assessment is critical for many language arts outcomes, especially for writing outcomes. Students benefit when they use specific criteria to assess their own performances as well as the performances of other students. Therefore, in unit plans, teachers should emphasize student involvement in assessment.

34

Practical Applications of an Outcomes Emphasis

The following Grade 5–6 writing scenario, developed by a colleague, illustrates the power of program modification and of varied groupings for instruction.

Background information

It is midway through the school year. Classroom procedures and routines are well established and students are comfortable working in different groupings. Through modeling and role playing students have developed the skills and language necessary for productive sharing in group settings. The teacher has decided to use analytic scoring on a recent piece of student writing to confirm informal observations and to direct further teaching.

From the analytic scoring and the resulting "Can Do" lists, the teacher is able to propose an instructional focus for each student's writing. A critical area of need for instruction for seven students lies in fluency and content. For another group of 12 average to above-average writers, the instructional focus would be on the use of vocabulary to improve their writing. (Four other students in the class show exceptional use of vocabulary in their writing and could serve, from time to time, as models or group leaders.) Another group, of 10 creative students who have a wealth of ideas for writing, needs to focus on editing skills as a means to improve the clarity of their ideas. Members of this group should take more ownership for the quality of their writing. There are 29 students in the class.

Planning group work

Establish focus groups. (For the needs analysed in the above example, three focus groups would be appropriate.)

Group 1: Fluency and content/organization (7 students)
Work on strategies for developing and elaborating on ideas.

Group 2: Vocabulary development (12 students)
Offer large-group modeling with short follow-up activities.
Provide small-group practice.

Group 3: Editing skills to improve the use of conventions (10 students)
Brainstorm and record a list of criteria for editing.
Use recent student samples for practice (with permission).
Students trade drafts and read strictly as editors using established criteria set by the group. (Encourage students to focus on usage as well as on capitals, punctuation and spelling.)
Provide practice sheets on use of modifiers, subject-verb correspondence, and so on.

Note: The concurrent running of several focus groups is an end point of optimum instruction. Teachers could start with the large group focused on vocabulary development and occasionally pull a small group for fluency and content instruction. Writing instruction will run in 45-minute periods, three days per week.

Day One: The teacher will work with the entire class during the first lesson.

• Explain how groupings were determined using a graph on the overhead to show strengths and needs of the class.
• Introduce the new focus groups and invite students to place themselves in groups based on their own self-assessment. (They will share this ranking individually and privately with the teacher.)

- Explain that vocabulary will be a sub-focus for all the groups. (Having fun with words will serve as the unifying element for the whole class groupings.)
- Read the first two paragraphs from "A Worn Path" by Eudora Welty as an example of the powerful use of vocabulary.
- Assign the vocabulary activity below. (While students are working on it, call up individual students to confirm their membership in a focus group.)
- VOCABULARY ACTIVITY: Students will work as partners to brainstorm descriptive words about a baby learning to walk, a group of boys or girls playing kickball, an embarrassing moment, a playful kitten.
- Ask students to write a short descriptive paragraph on each one of the above experiences.

Day Two: The teacher will review procedures and expectations for group activities and set up assignments for groups.

Group 1	Group 2	Group 3
Students will first work with the teacher, then independently.	Students will work independently.	Students will first work independently, then with the teacher.
After brainstorming and working through the activity, students will choose 3 of their 8 ideas and do a 7–10 minute fast write on each. (When students are working on fast writes, the teacher checks on group 2 and helps group 3 set up an editing criteria list.)	• Students will use the Day One vocabulary exercise as a jumping off point for improving their writing. • Each student may choose to write either (a) a character description or (b) a description of a setting to establish mood.	• Each student will trade a piece of recent writing with another group member and read it over to find ideas for editing criteria. • With the teacher, the group will create an editing criteria list.

continued

Day Two *(continued)*

Group 1	Group 2	Group 3
	• Before the students start to write they will have an opportunity to read examples from recent literature they have studied (photocopied by teacher).	

Day Three: The teacher will set up directions and procedures.

Group 2	Group 3	Group 1
Students will first work with the teacher, then independently.	Students will first work independently, then with the teacher.	Students will work independently, while the teacher checks/observes.
(The teacher observes that students are using mostly adjectives to enhance their descriptive writing and plans to introduce a lesson on verbs.)	• Students will begin editing a common piece (created by the teacher to provide controlled errors), using their established criteria. • Students will do a grammar practice worksheet focusing on consistent tense. • The teacher will work with the group to assess their editing. • If necessary, the teacher will model proofreading strategies.	Students will pair off and do an oral elaboration on one of their fast writes to determine if they have enough information. (If so, they should write; if not, they should return to quick writes or lists for other ideas.)

Day Four: The teacher will respond to Day Three observation of group 2 by introducing a "Fun with Words" activity intended to promote the use of strong verbs. The teacher will work with the whole class in order to encourage and model for reluctant writers, and to help average and advanced writers improve.

FOLLOW-UP: Group 1 (fluency) Can use ideas on verbs to enhance their writing in progress.

Group 2 (vocabulary) Can use list of strong verbs to improve their descriptive writing in progress.

Group 3 (editing) Can save activity notes for next piece of writing.

Day Five: The teacher will direct group activities.

Group 1: Once the students have a topic that they feel they can elaborate on, switch the focus from fluency to organization of ideas.

Group 2: Once the students have developed an awareness of vocabulary in their short descriptive pieces, invite them to begin a new piece of writing, keeping what they have learned in mind.

Group 3: Once the students have begun to edit more consistently, request that they begin a new piece of writing, keeping their editing criteria in mind.

The above model suggests how group work permits direct instruction in those skill areas where students need most help if they are to meet outcomes. I have found value in following tested guidelines for group work.

PRACTICAL GUIDELINES FOR SMALL-GROUP WORK

1. Begin with groups of two or three; work with larger groups later.

2. Specify the time allowed for small-group work; for students who are unskilled in group work, begin with shorter time periods.

3. Always require specific action following small-group work, perhaps a brief written or oral report.

4. Encourage students to begin their small-group work by articulating and agreeing upon their interpretation of the group's task.

5. Vary your use of self-selected and assigned groups throughout the year; students should learn that small groups dissolve when the task is completed and that different groups form for different tasks.

6. Encourage students to use self-assessment checklists to monitor their work in small-group activities and to establish goals for their small-group work.

7. Before students' first experience with small-group work, review your rationale and expectations.

The facing form, on page 41, excerpted from my book *Student Self-Assessment: A Powerful Process for Helping Students Revise Their Writing*, has been employed successfully by many students and teachers and may prove useful when you introduce focus groups for instruction.

SMALL-GROUP WORK
STUDENT ASSESSMENT FORM

Criteria	My Goals for Small-Group Work

_____ 1. I helped the group
review its task.

_____ 2. I contributed relevant
ideas; I stayed on topic.

_____ 3. I listened carefully to
other group members.

_____ 4. I was open-minded about
different interpretations
or understandings.

_____ 5. I helped the group stay
focused on its task.

_____ 6. I contributed to the
summary which concluded
the group work.

_____ 7. I encouraged all members
of the group to contribute.

PROFESSIONAL DEVELOPMENT FOCUS:
Refining Unit to Meet Student Needs

• Review one of your language arts units to refine your plans for
program modification and for varied grouping of students.

CHAPTER 3

Assessment, Standards and Reporting Practice

Balanced Assessment

Perhaps the truest measure of any curriculum is not what expectations it lists in documents, but rather what influence it exerts on the assessment of learning. In education as in life, we assess what we value. How will an outcomes focus affect the assessment of language learning? To explore the importance of this question, let's consider the assessment implications of outcomes such as the following ones for Grade 3, each appearing in a different, recently prescribed, outcomes-based language arts curriculum:

- uses correct subject-verb agreement

- knows and uses some punctuation conventions, including periods, exclamation marks and questions marks, when editing and proofreading

Will Grade 3 students be expected to pass a subject-verb agreement test or a test in which they insert punctuation in pre-set sentences? Or, will they be expected to demonstrate these outcomes in their own writing? If so, the form and quality of assessment are quite different; so are the form and quality of the entire language arts curriculum.

The second example from a recently prescribed curriculum document sounds a clearer assessment message than does the first. Its use of the words "editing" and "proofreading" indicates that students should demonstrate their ability to punctuate in their own writing. One might assume that students would also be revising for word choices, organization, sentence patterns, and content. In the first instance, however, students would be completing a pre-specified response assessment, the requirement that they replicate a predetermined correct answer. The second outcome calls for a more complex performance assessment in which students would apply usage conventions in their own writing.

If we accept the principle that mandated programs ought to direct the assessment of students, language arts teachers should ensure that the assessment is appropriate and comprehensive. For the usage outcomes cited above, performance assessment, in which students demonstrate the outcome in their own writing, is clearly appropriate. Teachers should ensure that if forms of standardized assessment are used in their school, district, province or state, the assessment squares with the mandated language arts program. If it does not, probably because of an isolated subskills emphasis, teachers should work through professional organizations to discourage such inappropriate practice.

With its life skills accent, an outcomes-based language arts program implies an emphasis on performance assessments. Language arts programs that require students to apply, rather than to recall knowledge, to compose rather than to complete worksheets, to consider various solutions to problems, to research, to communicate personal understandings and interpretations — important themes in both outcomes and language arts professional literature — nudge educators to performance assessment.

Performance assessment demands the application of criteria to judge an activity or product which cannot be predicted beforehand. Examples of learning activities that require performance assessment include acting, the composition and performance of music, artistic composition, problem solving, research, readers' theatre, debating, oral interpretation of literature, audiovisual presentations, and, of course, writing.

Criteria to assess performances should be worded as specifically as possible. For example "good descriptive content" is less helpful than criteria such as the following:

• The description conveys a single dominant impression.
• The description contains details that suggest the dominant impression.
• The description contains details that are original or unusual.

- The description contains words that connote the dominant impression.

Criteria are most effectively developed when teachers review the critical features of actual student performances, identify those features in the performances and separate features that distinguish extraordinary from standard and substandard performances. Textual resources are often helpful in articulating the specific criteria required for the fair and appropriate assessment of performances. Some departments of education, notably Alberta Education, have developed assessment forms that offer precise descriptions of desirable performance in writing.

While balanced assessment in language arts emphasizes performance assessment, it includes two other types of assessment too. These are pre-specified response assessment where, for example, students paraphrase main ideas presented in an article or oral presentation and observational assessment where the teacher might see how, in a small-group discussion, a student is staying on topic, contributing relevant information, helping the group focus, and summarizing ideas. Two books that are particularly helpful in balancing language arts assessment are *Marking Success*, by Neil Graham and Jerry George, and *Hitting the Mark: Assessment Tools for Teachers*, by Don Aker. Each of these books offers practical advice and examples of assessment forms.

Finally, balanced assessment includes the assessment of group work. With its life skills emphasis, an outcomes curriculum should honor the assessment of a group's performances as well as that of an individual student. Success in the workplace frequently demands collaborative effort, so assessment restricted to individual assessment is out-of-date. While assessment of group performances is not new in language arts programs, it is supported and emphasized by the outcomes perspective.

- Review the language arts expectations specified for the grade(s) that you teach. Use a "P" to indicate outcomes that are most appropriately assessed through a performance assessment, a "PS" to indicate outcomes that are most appropriately assessed through pre-specified response, and an "O" to indicate outcomes that are most appropriately assessed through observation.

- Place a check mark beside outcomes that might best be assessed during or following collaborative effort by students.

Formative Assessment of Learning

The implementation of any revised language arts program is an appropriate time to review principles of effective formative assessment. Formative assessment invites improvement in subsequent work. It thereby complements "summative" assessment, which is a final judgment about student achievement. When the assessment of learning is primarily formative, students learn most effectively what they need to succeed when summative assessments are required. While accountability is a critical purpose for assessment, advancing students' learning should always be the primary purpose.

An outcomes perspective, with its emphasis on improved student learning, amplifies the characteristics of effective formative assessment. The following characteristics are essential if evaluation is to be more useful to students than the mere assignment of a mark.

1. The learner should receive specific advice on how to improve subsequent performances of learning.

2. The learner should be actively engaged in self-assessment and · goal setting related to all performances of learning.

3. The learner should receive praise for accomplishments as well as challenges for future learning.

4. The learner should receive regular feedback.

5. The learner should receive clearly expressed feedback.

6. The learner should clearly understand methods and emphases selected for assessment.

PROFESSIONAL DEVELOPMENT FOCUS:
Fostering Constructive Assessment

- Explain how you plan to incorporate some of the characteristics of formative assessment in your students' language arts program.

Reporting of Student Progress in Language Arts

An outcomes perspective clearly implies that students be assessed according to expectations specified for their grade or level. A corollary is that report cards present honest evaluations of student progress related to these expectations. Always be sure to inform parents when such grade-specific assessment is not being followed in the best interests of their child. For purposes of this discussion, "assessment" refers to the activities selected to determine the extent of student learning of prescribed outcomes or expectations. "Evaluation" refers to the judgments made about the extent of a particular student's learning of prescribed outcomes or expectations.

How should students be assessed when they are progressing, but are not meeting the expectations for their grade? Should English as a Second Language (ESL) students receive Fs until their language proficiency is at grade level? Should students on modified or parallel programs receive Fs? These questions require attention as part of the implementation of outcomes-inspired curricula.

An enlightened approach to reporting student progress is *always* to assess and to report student progress according to outcomes which are appropriate for the child. ESL students and students in modified and parallel programs are entitled to top grades when their progress warrants top grades.

Parents need to know when their children are channeled into modified or parallel programs. Many jurisdictions require an

Individual Program Plan (IPP), developed by both parents and teachers, when the gap between a student's level of achievement and the grade placement is wide. Parents should know generally how the program compares to grade-level expectations. Some jurisdictions employ a coding on report cards, such as "M" or "MP" for Modified Program, when the child is not working at grade level.

Teachers should strive to be as specific as possible in informing parents about modified or parallel programs and in inviting them to cooperate in the child's education. You might discuss instructional focus, which may be skills and strategies; materials; time allotments; complementary assistance from other adults or peers; the setting for learning; and, of course, assessment.

On a related topic, an outcomes perspective should encourage schools to adopt reporting procedures that include students. These activities include student-led conferences, student participation in parent-teacher interviews and student preparation of their own written reports to parents to complement those prepared by the teacher.

PROFESSIONAL DEVELOPMENT FOCUS:
Improving Reporting to Parents

- Assess the adequacy of your students' report card forms and of current reporting procedures for the expectations in your currently prescribed language arts program.

- Discuss how your school could enhance its effectiveness in communicating student progress to parents.

- Consider how important parent-teacher conferences are in complementing information presented in your students' report cards.

Student Self-Assessment

The outcomes influence on any curriculum which demands performance assessment nudges educators toward student self-assessment. In an earlier book, *Student Self-Assessment: A Powerful Strategy for Helping Students Improve Their Writing*, I stressed that student writing improves when students learn to apply specific and appropriate criteria to revise their writing. Other educators have documented the power of student self-assessment for performance expectations beyond writing. Once again, performance expectations are those which demand artistic work which cannot be precisely predicted. Such work can be appropriately assessed only through application of specific criteria related to the purpose, audience, form, content and technical qualities of the performance.

When students engage in self-assessment related to any performance, they internalize expectations for their performance and take ownership of their learning. Outcomes advocates would be pleased to note that frequent student self-assessment results in improved performances, as documented in my earlier book and in research on writing summarized by George Hillocks: "As a group these studies conclude rather clearly that engaging young writers in the use of criteria, applied to their own and each other's writing, results not only in more effective writing but in superior first drafts" (*Research on Written Composition, New Directions for Teaching*, p. 160). Writing is certainly a performance. The content of any composition cannot be precisely predicted and only through application of relevant criteria can it be appropriately assessed.

The following principles are critical if students are to become skilful in self-assessment to benefit performances in their learning:

- Before students first engage in self-assessment with specific criteria, teachers should model the process.
- Students should engage in self-assessment with criteria related to their personal learning goals as well as with criteria related to performance expectations.
- Rather than simply presenting performance criteria to students, teachers should encourage students to develop performance criteria. Students can usefully discuss the features of a successful performance before they perform and assess their own performances.
- When students inaccurately or inappropriately apply a criterion in self-assessment, teachers view the faulty self-assessment as a "teachable moment" — an opportunity to review the desirable quality in the performance.

Here is an example of a self-assessment form prepared for a specific type of writing, namely, description. The form highlights many, but certainly not all, features which typify effective description. Teachers can modify such self-assessment forms according to the needs and abilities of students in the class. The blanks beside numbers 8 and 9 on this one invite students to add self-assessment criteria related to their personal writing goals.

CRITERIA FOR SELF-ASSESSMENT:
Description

Check relevant criteria.

_____ 1. The dominant impression conveyed by my description is _____

_____ 2. I have checked that I have suggested but have not directly stated the dominant impression.
_____ yes _____ no

_____ 3. The details that most effectively suggest the dominant impression are _____ ,
_____, and
_____

_____ 4. By placing details in the order I have selected, I am emphasizing _____

_____ 5. The most unusual detail is _____

_____ 6. My most imaginative images (word pictures) are
_____ , _____,
and _____

_____ 7. My most colorful words are _____ ,
_____, and _____

_____ 8. _____
_____
_____

_____ 9. _____
_____
_____

The following form related to student goal setting can be translated into a "Can Do" and "Need to Do" list for younger students. Many students have used a similar form as the first page of a work collection or a portfolio. Once again, an outcomes emphasis supports student goal setting and self-monitoring since these activities foster ownership of one's learning.

MY LANGUAGE ARTS GOALS

NAME: _____   DATE: _____

GRADE: _____

FROM _____ TO_____

               Date   Date

GOALS ACHIEVED	GOALS STILL TO BE ACHIEVED

PROFESSIONAL DEVELOPMENT FOCUS:
Developing a Self-Assessment Form

• Possibly with the cooperation of your students, develop a student self-assessment form which students can employ for a language arts performance — an oral language performance, a visual communication performance, or a writing performance.

Rubrics and Exemplars

Rubrics are scoring guides employed for the assessment of any performance task, including writing. They possess two important characteristics:

- a specific itemization of critical features in the performance;
- a description of levels or gradations of the quality of the performance, that is, from high to low quality.

While rubrics are typically used in large-scale assessments, they are valuable for classroom assessment as well. From an outcomes perspective, they are especially useful. That is because they clearly communicate expectations to students and parents. One valuable form of student self-assessment is for students to work with the same rubric employed by the teacher to assess a performance.

Students frequently benefit from cooperating with their teacher to develop a scoring rubric for a performance at hand. One advantage of this approach is that such a rubric tends to be worded comprehensibly for students. While the following rubric, developed by a colleague, illustrates the two important characteristics of rubrics, it also emphasizes that language arts performances often extend beyond writing and oral language. Several current textbooks and professional references suggest that students create dioramas in response to literature.

Page 50 of this book featured a self-assessment form for descriptive writing. The scoring rubric on pages 54 and 55 could be used for summative assessment of descriptive writing.

Note the analytical rather than the holistic format of the rubric. An analytical design leads to scoring in critical categories. It permits differentiated feedback for the writer (or performer) through separate scores for the different categories. A holistic design presents a single descriptor for each score; it permits speed in marking since each paper receives only one score. Teachers committed to formative assessment will emphasize analytical scoring rubrics which are close to the self-assessment forms used by students. In designing rubrics for writing-in-progress, teachers will find guidance in those composition textbooks and handbooks which identify critical features for different writing forms.

Rubrics are inadequate for establishing and communicating standards — they tell, but do not show. They work most effectively with exemplars, or illustrations of performances at various levels of quality. Exemplars can be print samples, artistic representations, and audiotaped or videotaped performances. From an outcomes perspective, teachers are wise to present exemplars to students and to encourage them to relate the exemplars to assessment rubrics.

RUBRIC: Diorama Project

Name:_____ Date:_____

ORIGINALITY / DESIGN	1	2	3	4

1. Little design originality is evident.
2. Good design originality is evident.
3. Very good and innovative design originality is evident.
4. Excellent and innovative design originality is evident.

CRAFTSMANSHIP (Use of materials)	1	2	3	4

1. Very little craftsmanship is evident.
2. Good craftsmanship is evident.
3. Very good craftsmanship is evident.
4. Excellent craftsmanship is evident.

EFFORT	1	2	3	4

1. Very little effort is evident.
2. Good effort.
3. Very good effort.
4. Excellent effort (consistently tried to work and complete the task at hand).

MEANING	1	2	3	4

1. The theme or topic is not very well visually represented.
2. Visual representation of theme or topic is adequate.
3. Visual representation of theme or topic is very good.
4. Visual representation of theme or topic is excellent.

RUBRIC: Descriptive Writing

CONTENT AND ORGANIZATION

∞
- The student's writing consistently and clearly implies a dominant impression.
- The student's writing contains unique and specific details to suggest the dominant impression.
- The student's organization of detail clearly emphasizes a dominant impression.

❸
- The student's writing suggests a dominant impression.
- The student's writing contains specific details to suggest the dominant impression.
- The student's organization of detail somewhat emphasizes a dominant impression.

❷
- The student's writing is inconsistent in its suggestion of a dominant impression.
- The student's writing contains general details to suggest the dominant impression.
- The student's organization of detail vaguely emphasizes a dominant impression.

❶
- The student's writing suggests no particular dominant impression.
- The student's writing contains unfocused, unspecific detail.
- The student's organization of detail hardly emphasizes a dominant impression.

VOICE AND TECHNIQUE

∞
- The student's vocabulary and imagery are consistently connotative of the dominant impression.
- The student's writing consistently reflects a clear voice which expresses an emotional response.

❸
- The student's vocabulary and imagery are often connotative of the dominant impression.
- The student's writing reflects a clear voice which expresses an emotional response.

RUBRIC: Descriptive Writing

VOICE AND TECHNIQUE (*continued*)

❷
- The student's vocabulary and imagery are appropriate but ordinary.
- The student's writing reflects an inconsistent or uncontrolled voice related to an emotional response.

❶
- The student's vocabulary and imagery are not carefully chosen for connotative effect.
- The student's writing expresses no particular voice related to an emotional response.

SYNTAX AND USAGE

∞
- The student's writing contains sentence patterns (possibly sentence fragments) related to the dominant impression.
- The student's writing demonstrates consistently correct usage.

❸
- The student's writing contains acceptable sentence patterns (possibly sentence fragments) related to the dominant impression.
- The student's writing contains relatively few errors in usage which do not distract the reader from the dominant impression.

❷
- The student's writing demonstrates limited control of sentence patterns related to the dominant impression.
- The student's writing contains errors in usage which distract the reader from the dominant impression.

❶
- The student's writing demonstrates no control of sentence patterns related to the dominant impression.
- The student's writing contains so many errors in usage that the reader is constantly distracted from a sense of dominant impression.

Rubrics complemented by exemplars clearly improve student performance. The achievement and diploma examination programs in Alberta offer powerful evidence of this. As part of its assessment program of writing, Alberta Education regularly publishes rubrics and exemplars of student writing at various levels of competence. In 1990, an Alberta Education study compared student writing in two English and one social studies course between 1984 and 1990. The study concluded that papers judged to be satisfactory were significantly better in 1990 than in 1984. Alberta Education's 1994 achievement-test publication of Grade 9 student writing-samples indicates that the overall quality of the writing in English language arts in 1994 was superior to that composed in 1990. From an outcomes perspective, these studies are important in their message that rubrics and exemplars help teachers and students improve the quality of written performances. Telling without showing is inferior pedagogy!

Two exemplars that apply to Grade 9 descriptive writing follow. Throughout this chapter, I have used descriptive writing to illustrate points about performance criteria, student self-assessment, rubrics and now exemplars. Future Grade 9 language arts students will probably benefit in their descriptive writing if they consider and suggest improvements to exemplars such as these.

On My Bike

The moisture-deprived fall air evaporated the perspiration on my wind-swept face, as I raced headlong down the dusty gravel path. Despite the delapitated condition of the bike on which I sat, I still hugged corners, like a hovercraft skimming the breakers, with a rush of adrenaline, a rush that could be provided by few other activities. As the dead leaves became even deader with a crunch, crinkle, snap, and I rocketed further down the twisted abyss of speed and motion, my overworked heart pulsated more labourously. An unavoidable weariness begun to hang over me, like a dark storm cloud, heavy with thunder. My aching hamstrings, and overheated body were not what they were 5 minutes ago . . . had it been 5 minutes? it seemed like centuries. So I hopped off my bike, and wondered why I had been compelled to get on in the first place.

The Volleyball Game

The loud, enthusiastic crowd bursts into an uproar, filling the stuffy, stale smelling gym with noise. People on the sidelines bobbing up and down, up and down cheering on their players. The home team sends the ball hurtling over the net, sending the herd of fans once again into utter mayhem. Beads of sweat drip down the players faces, all of them a bit uneasy and feeling the pressure. Six hot, perspiring bodies scatter throughout the court, ready for anything that is sent their way. Sliding to the right and then to the left, quick and swift like a lightning bolt darting across an open field. Total focus on the round object being propelled over the net. The players' look is one of pure concentration and deter-mination, similar to that of a wild cat ready to pounce on its prey. Growing goose bumps on the observer's arms . . . next point wins. The ball is contacted and sent into flight over the net; a hush falls over the crowd. Bump, set, spike, the ball is forced downwards, moving at tremendous speed towards the nearing gym floor. THUD! It strikes the solid ground. The gym, erupts with celebra-tion, cheering fans and team members hit the roof with complete satisfaction and delight. Ahhh, the sweet taste of victory!

These exemplars, completed by students using word-proces-sors, would certainly receive high ratings on the rubric presented earlier. Both pieces create dominant impressions. They contain interesting and unique details — inspired, no doubt, by direct observation of the event and experience described. In "On My Bike" words such as "rocketed" and "pulsated" connote speed and excitement as do images such as "raced headlong down the gravel path" and "hugged corners, like a hovercraft skimming the break-ers." In "The Volleyball Game," words such as "scatter" and "propelled" suggest the action and excitement of the match. The image of the "wildcat ready to pounce" underlines the game's tension. While both exemplars contain minor errors in usage — spelling and apostrophe errors — these are not distracting to the reader.

Classes could employ exemplars such as these in a variety of ways. Students could be challenged to comment on features that make the pieces effective and to suggest alternatives. Through this activity, the teacher notes critical features on the blackboard and, in effect, creates a self-assessment form for students to use in their own writing. Students could also be challenged to use a self-assessment form or rubric to assess the exemplar. Since rubrics are often jargon-ridden, teachers who use the approach would ensure that students understand points on the rubric. Throughout work with exemplars, teachers stress that student exemplars should be honored, that suggestions for improvement of exemplars should always be constructive.

As previously mentioned, NCTE's *Standards Consensus Series* and Alberta Education's *Classroom Assessment Materials Program* are valuable resources based on large-scale school assessments of writing. A series entitled *Writing Sense: Your Writing Skills Handbook*, with separate handbooks for Grades 4, 5, and 6, is also impressive in its presentation of student exemplars related to selected writing forms.

PROFESSIONAL DEVELOPMENT FOCUS:
Preparing to Use a Rubric

- Possibly with the cooperation of your students, develop a rubric for a performance project that some or all of your students will complete.

- Collect exemplars that illustrate the different ratings of the rubric that you have developed.

Use of Exemplars by Classroom Teachers

Exemplars, when used with rubrics, are such powerful instructional resources that teachers should collect their own for a variety of performances, including writing. These exemplars can be photocopies of work samples, photographs, audiotapes, and videotapes. Sometimes, students are willing to donate original work done for class as an instructional resource for next year's students. Teachers from all grade levels should gather exemplars that relate to their students' program.

The following descriptions of classroom practice testify about the value of exemplars, especially when combined with rubrics and self-assessment.

Example one: Grade 3

A Grade 2 teacher has used exemplars and rubrics as an instructional resource for writing for several years. The teacher began her work with exemplars when she taught Grade 3. Her early success with the practice has motivated her to employ it to instruct Grade 2 student writers as well.

For all narrative writing in her Grade 3 class, the teacher based her instruction on the five-point rubric published by Alberta Education for Grade 3 achievement-test writing. First, the teacher engaged students in relevant pre-writing and drafting work. After the writing of the first draft, she invited students to work with one or two exemplars — stories completed by her previous Grade 3 students. She did not present students with a copy of a narrative writing rubric, but highlighted criteria related to the content, organization, sentence structure, vocabulary and usage from it throughout the year in her presentation of the exemplars.

The teacher first focused on details which help the reader visualize the story. Students pointed out helpful details as a prelude to revising their own writing for details which would help the reader see and understand. The teacher went on to employ a similar approach with Grade 3 report writing and poetry writing. In addition, she used videotaped exemplars to illustrate desirable features in readers' theatre.

The teacher notes that she always uses exemplars to focus students' attention on a particular element in writing or in a performance. In addition, she stresses the value in having students work with exemplars of varying quality, ordinary and extraordinary. Sometimes, she challenges students to indicate why one composition succeeds more than another.

When asked about the benefits of her students' work with exemplars, the teacher indicated that, in revision activities, students find the work of other students more motivating than that of professional writers. Students seem to be less intimidated when they note what other students can do. The teacher quoted a remark they frequently made. "I can do even better than that in my own story." The teacher believes that because of students' work with exemplars and criteria, the overall quality of student writing improves from year to year.

Here is a writing sample which the teacher shared early in her first year of work with exemplars. The sample, the work of a previous Grade 3 student, was employed with more recent classes to focus students on narrative details that help the reader visualize.

One hot summer day I was playing with my brother and my cousin in our wooden tree fort. We were playing house. My brother was a dog, my cousin was an old man, and I was the owner of the dog. My brother was rubbing his neck on the floor of our fort because it was itchy and he got a big sliver by the floor. My brother was crying and lots of blood was coming out of his neck going on to the floor. My cousin quickly ran and got my mom and when my cousin went to get my mom lots of blood was coming out. My brother was crying a lot too. When my cousin and mom came out we all felt frightened. Then we took my brother to the doctor's and he got four stitches. When we got home he didn't get to play till the next day.

Following discussion about effective details in the exemplar and about details which could be added, the teacher encouraged students to work with a partner to add helpful details to their first drafts. The following sample reflects how one student who has used exemplars has improved the detail in her narrative writing.

The Bad Racoon

One warm night in August my dad, my grandma, my papa and I were camping in Olds. My mom didn't come with us. My grandma and papa were sleeping in the motorhome but me and my dad were sleeping in tents. Before we had dinner we all went to the park. I went down the side a lot. We had ribs, corn, salad, and soup. We had a nice dinner it was very good. After supper we rosted marshmellows over the fire. While we were eating roasted marshmellows we told scary stories. Then we went to bed. At about 12:00 A.M. A racoon came into my tent. It got into my tent because I left my tent open. The racoon bit my toe. It hurt and I cried. At first when I wasn't really awake I thught it was my cats ET. or Oilver, because before my cats had bit me. When I found out it was a racoon I screamed for dad I said "DAD HELP!!" He took me to the hospital. Then my dad went back to the camping ground. My dad took a cookie sheet and his gloves and picked up the racoon and put him on the cookie sheet and threw him out into the forest. I had to stay at the hospital for two days. Mom guessed that dad put him on a cookie sheet. "Ah ha ha ha" said my mom. "Did you have to go to the Hospital?" "Yes I did Mom but that's another story." " Are the cats ok?" "Yes they are." "Well I bet your happy to sleep in your own bed now." "Yes I am!" The End

Although, this story could certainly be improved, it demonstrates commitment to narrative detail. The teacher believed strongly that the work with exemplars benefited the student.

Example two: Grades 4, 5, and 6

A teacher who serves in a language arts curriculum support position in her District became so convinced about the importance of specific revision criteria and exemplars for writing forms that she coordinated a project involving teachers from Grades 4, 5, and 6. As part of her initiative, she also visits classes to model effective work with revision criteria and exemplars. Teachers in the District can concur that student work with models and criteria improves student writing.

The following excerpt from related writing by the language arts curriculum leader features self-assessment criteria followed by exemplars of effective literature-response writing.

- **CONTENT**

❏ Did I identify the book I read?
❏ Does my response include some of the following:

_____ predictions
_____ opinions (*likes or dislikes*)
_____ comparisons to my life
_____ illustrations
_____ observations
_____ feelings
_____ reflections
_____ descriptions
_____ author's style (*character development, setting, plot, sentence patterns, choice of words*)

- **ORGANIZATION**

❑ Are my ideas in a logical order?

- **SENTENCE STRUCTURE**

❑ Have I used complete sentences?
❑ Have I avoided run-on sentences?

- **VOCABULARY**

❑ Have I chosen words that are precise and colorful?

- **CONVENTIONS**

❑ Are all my words spelled correctly?
❑ Does my punctuation help the meaning of my story?
❑ Have I used correct capitalization and punctuation?

Literature Response Examples

EXAMPLE #1   From *Could Dracula Live in Woodford?*

Well, I didn't think that this was exciting or funny or anything like that. But I sure was happy that they got Sam back. What happened was that Jennie and Beth had frantically run home, worrying about Sam and thinking that something terrible was going to happen to her. Just think how worried you'd be if Sam was your dog and she was in a horrible place similar to McIver's old dilapidated shack. I would be worried if she was my dog. That's for sure.

While they were running home, Jennie and Beth started to think about how they would get Sam out of the basement. They came up with an idea that was sure to work. They took a large board from Beth's garage and lowered it into the opened window of the cellar. Jennie made a delivery from the drugstore and kept Mr. McIver occupied while Beth managed to sneak her way to the side of the house and get Sam out through the window.

I thought their plan to rescue Sam was pretty ingenious and daring considering that they thought that Mr. McIver was a vampire. I did think however that Sam was the bravest one because she allowed herself to get trapped in the basement so that Jennie and Beth could save themselves.

EXAMPLE #2   From *Could Dracula Live in Woodford?*

Sam hated Woodford so much, that she spent her first few days living there thinking about how she would run away. Talk about unhappy. Sam must really like her old neighborhood a lot if she wants to get back that badly! Jennie too was just as sad as Sam, moping around about Sarah moving away for a reason that they do not tell in the book. It would only make sense to tell the reader. Oh, by the way, did I mention that Jennie used to call Sam "Mop Dog" before she found out her real name. Weird!

Following her classroom work with specific criteria and exemplars, the support teacher typically receives letters from students in the class. The following letters indicate that at least some students appreciate learning about writing through exemplars.

Dear Miss Prince:

Thank for taking time to teach us all the wonderful stuff this morning. Now I can write even better I think that we shoud continue this progress because now I don't have to complain about the marks I get because I'll know why I get them. Your a great L.A. teacher!

Sincerely,

Beth Henson

Dear Miss Prince:

I thought that today I really learned how hard it is to be a teacher. It was hard to make a decision on some of the stories but I found it to be fun. There were 2 stories that I enjoyed but one was imposible to understand. It was very interesting what we did. I hope you can come again. Now I understand what I should right and how. Now I also know what the teacher expects from me, all I thought was that you (other teachers) expected was our best try.

Sincerely,

Mary O'Malley

Indeed, to advance student writing ability, teachers must do more than expect students' "best try." Teachers should present exemplars and should engage students in thoughtful self-assessment with criteria related to these exemplars. Doing so will enable students to improve their writing.

Example three: Junior high

After never considering exemplars as an instructional resource in his first years of teaching, a junior high language arts teacher intuitively sensed their value to junior high school writers more than eight years ago. The teacher employs photocopies of work samples and videotapes of oral presentations for a variety of work, including student poetry, student-created advertising, character sketches, narrative writing, and an annual project entitled "A Report Card on My Parent." For several years, the teacher has had Grade 8 students write and illustrate children's books, too.

The teacher prefers an inductive approach to generate rubrics. Working with exemplars, students identify features which make the performance (including writing) successful. Sometimes, the teacher plans for students to analyse exceptional and ordinary work samples. He challenges his students to identify those features which separate the exceptional from the ordinary performance. Students later self-assess their own work for these features.

The teacher is unequivocal in his advocacy of the approach. Over the years of his work with exemplars, he has noticed a steady improvement in student work. Furthermore, he has noted that struggling students benefit most from exemplars. These students often amaze themselves and their parents with performances inspired by exemplars.

The following excerpts from children's stories written by the teacher's Grade 8 students underline the power of exemplars. The first excerpt represents the best story written by the teacher's students before he introduced exemplars.

Hello, my name is Timmy. I'd like to tell you about the dinosaur that lived in my back yard. Nobody knows about my dinosaur except for my family and me. So keep it a secret! . . .

Eight years later, the teacher works with a library of children's stories written by several Grade 8 students. He notes that the best children's stories of his first attempt with a class would now rank among the weakest in his current class. The following excerpt of a first page represents an improved sense of story form and a much more impressive command of language.

> *In the valley, the little town of Binkeyville was calm as Junior sat on top of Nulls Hill. The remarkable tree on top of the enormous hill was swaying in the wind. The hand-sized leaves provided shade for Junior as he thought for hours until his head throbbed.*
>
> *His gray eyes glistened in the sun as he stared into the light, blue sky. His blond hair was tangled in the misty grass as he lay there under his favorite tree. His plump arms were crossed behind his head. Colorful butterflies rested on the tall dandelions and Junior quietly observed them.*
>
> *Junior often went to the center of this quaint town to think. He had been given a project by his teacher, Mrs. Gush, to research a topic of his choice. He was to write a five page report with his findings. Junior thought this project was going to be difficult. After all, he was only in the fourth grade.*

Example four: Senior high

A senior high school English teacher works in a school in which the development of rubrics and exemplars has been an expectation since the school opening a few years ago. While agreeing that the use of rubrics and exemplars advances student learning, especially the work of struggling students, the teacher offers cautions about their use.

In striving to develop a collection of exemplars, the teacher has discovered that collecting exemplars that illustrate all of the desirable features described in a rubric is difficult. Often, exemplars will shine as illustrations of only one or two of several ideal features. Teachers are wise to take an ongoing, long-term perspective on collecting them.

The teacher also cautions that many students require frequent practice and the opportunity for multiple demonstrations of outcomes. He advises emphasizing important outcomes in rubrics and exemplars several times throughout the year. He also points out that rubrics and exemplars that work well with one class may be too advanced or too trivial for another at the same grade level. Obviously, while the best exemplars stretch students to improved performances, the performances must be reachable. Developing rubrics and presenting exemplars require ongoing work and adaptability to different classes.

The teacher argues that future textbooks and handbooks should feature more student work as exemplars. Textbooks and handbooks that rely exclusively on professional exemplars often frustrate students — the samples are far above reasonable expectations for them. The teacher argues that a balance between student exemplars and professional illustrations in a textbook or handbook would be more useful to students and teachers.

For the following rubric, "Levels of Performance for Shakespearean Drama — Group Project," the teacher collects videotaped exemplars of student performance.

COURSE: ENGLISH 30
SKILL (STRAND): Reading, Writing, Speaking
GENERIC UNIT: Shakespearean Drama
THEME UNIT:
SELECTED TITLE: *Hamlet*
OUTCOME FOR SHAKESPEAREAN DRAMA — GROUP PROJECT:

Students will demonstrate their understanding of the play (its characters, plot, and themes) and the language of the play, and their own communication skills by participating in **ONE** group dramatization, as follows (or as approved by the teacher):

1. **THE ROASTING OF HAMLET:** Each student will assume the identity of a character from the play and, at a mock dinner, roast Hamlet, the guest of honor; one member of the group must be Hamlet, who speaks last and rebuts each of the previous speakers with his own satirical comments.

2. **HAMLET: THE LAST GENERATION:** Students will create and enact a new (space) scenario in which the characters remain true to the names and characters of the original story while trying to deal with a space-age crisis.

3. **THE YOUNG AND THE RECKLESS (GENERAL PALACE):** Students will re-create the essential plot or sub-plot of the play and present it in the form and style of a modern TV soap opera episode.

4. **HAMLET AND *FRIENDS*:** A new situation comedy combining characters from the play with the relationship concepts of a well-known TV sitcom, "Home Improvement" and "Seinfeld" being examples.

5. **HAMLET: REMEMBRANCE OF THINGS PAST:** A few years after the death of Hamlet and the restoration of order in the Danish Kingdom, we are taken to visit each of the following characters who, through substantial monologues, share their personal recollections and understanding of Hamlet and the turbulent court events leading to his death: Marcellus, Voltimand, the First Player, the Grave Digger, the Priest, Osric, and Horatio.

6. **THE LIFE OF HAMLET:** A Monty Python version of selected scenes or of a condensation of the entire play.

7. **THE H-FILES:** An investigation into the paranormal events in and around Elsinore Castle.

EXEMPLAR:

Not yet available; the presentations listed above will be videotaped and, along with the scripts, will be available for future classes.

RUBRIC: Levels of Performance for Shakespearean Drama — Group Project

DESCRIPTIVE SCALE: Working range is from Minimal (50–64%) to Acceptable (65–79%) to Mastery (80% +). For each outcome, a detailed description of indicators is outlined. Performance levels less than minimal are Not Acceptable.

DESCRIPTIVE SCALE *Base Values:*	MINIMAL Re-assessment Required 50%	ACCEPTABLE Re-assessment Recommended 65%	MASTERY Re-assessment Not Required 80%
Outcome for Shakespearean Drama — Group Project Applies	**Reading:** The student's stated observations and/or actions, tone, and facial expressions show little real understanding of his/her character's values, motivations, and attitudes toward the other characters. **Writing:** A) Content: Ideas lack originality and few are chosen to focus on important character qualities. There may be some confusing gaps or inconsistencies in the sequence of the skit.	**Reading:** The student's stated observations and/or actions, tone, and facial expressions show the traditional understanding of his/her character's values, motivations, and attitudes toward the other characters. **Writing:** A) Content: Ideas are generally original and some details are carefully chosen to focus on important character qualities. There may be some gaps in the sequence of the skit.	**Reading:** The student's stated observations and/or actions, tone, and facial expressions show an insightful understanding of his/her character's values, motivations, and attitudes toward the other characters. **Writing:** A) Content: Ideas are original. Detail is carefully chosen to focus on important character qualities and to develop the plot of the sketch with no glaring gaps in the logical sequence of the skit.

RUBRIC: Levels of Performance for Shakespearean Drama — Group Project

DESCRIPTIVE SCALE: Working range is from Minimal (50 – 64%) to Acceptable (65 –79%) to Mastery (80% +). For each outcome, a detailed description of indicators is outlined. Performance levels less than minimal are Not Acceptable.

DESCRIPTIVE SCALE *Base Values:*	MINIMAL Re-assessment Required 50%	ACCEPTABLE Re-assessment Recommended 65%	MASTERY Re-assessment Not Required 80%
Outcome for Shakespearean Drama — Group Project Applies	B) Matters of Choice: The level of language is generally consistent with the scenario, but lacks wit or humor. C) Format: The script follows the model provided, but may not be clear or easily readable. **Speaking:** The student has attempted to memorize his/her lines for the skit, but may have to rely on notes or prompts to complete delivery. Delivery may be unclear or inaudible at times. Non-verbal factors have been mostly ignored or are distracting or inappropriate. The student has difficulty staying in character.	B) Matters of Choice: The level of language is usually consistent with the scenario and has some witty or funny parts. C) Format: The script mostly follows the model provided and is clear and readable. **Speaking:** The student has memorized his/her lines for the skit. Delivery is clear and audible, but there are some lapses in memory or tone. Non-verbal factors may not always support the dialogue. The student mostly stays in character.	B) Matters of Choice: The level of language usage is consistent with the chosen scenario and the dialogue is witty and funny. C) Format: The script follows exactly the prescribed model and is clear and easy to read. **Speaking:** The student has completely memorized his/her lines for the skit and delivers them clearly, audibly, and smoothly, with appropriate tone and no annoying lapses. Non-verbal factors, such as facial expressions and gestures, are always appropriate. The student stays in character.

Use of Rubrics and Exemplars in Large-Scale Assessments

In my professional development work with beginning teachers and with experienced teachers who are teaching language arts for the first time, I have noticed that their major concern has changed over the past few years. Four or five years ago, beginning teachers usually focused on resources and instructional activities. Now, in increasing numbers, they first ask about standards: "How do I know that my expectations are realistic?"

No doubt the concerns of these newly appointed language arts teachers is rooted in current controversies about whether students in selected jurisdictions are "measuring up." School jurisdictions and departments of education frequently mandate a standardized testing program to monitor student achievement. Unfortunately, these educational authorities sometimes publish results, even at the level of school comparisons. It is hardly surprising that standardized assessment raises the anxiety levels of beginning and experienced teachers alike.

Can such comparative assessments become a positive influence for best practice in language arts instruction? A few points seem relevant to issues about standards.

First, it is critical that beginning and experienced teachers develop and communicate their collegial understanding of expectations or standards. I usually advise beginning language arts teachers to talk to colleagues about the quality of a few selected writing samples before they first mark a set of papers. Furthermore, schools, school districts, and larger educational jurisdictions serve beginning teachers well by presenting them with exemplars of typical assignments as well as with rubrics and exemplars.

As part of a professional development program, teachers wisely engage in a standard-setting exercise for a variety of performance tasks, especially writing. The most certain method for consolidating an understanding of expectations is for teachers to talk about their assessment of selected samples of student work. An important part of their discussion focuses on assessment criteria or rubrics and on the selection of exemplars.

For the purposes of this book, large-scale assessment refers to that planned and implemented by someone other than the classroom teacher working independently. Frankly, for a shared understanding of standards or expectations, such large-scale assessment and group marking are required. Large-scale assessment should not be restricted to standardized tests imposed from on high! Neither need it always be external. Teachers have often told me that their most useful professional development has been the collegial development of assessment materials and the scoring of student work in a group setting with colleagues.

For all large-scale assessments, fundamental principles should be respected.

1. The assessment should be appropriate for curriculum outcomes. Therefore, for performance outcomes, performance assessment, including the development of rubrics and the selection of exemplars, is required.

2. As far as the setting of appropriate and realistic expectations go, classroom teachers should take a significant part in the development of large-scale assessment materials and in the marking of student work.

3. Towards reaching the goal of communicating standards and expectations, large-scale assessments should attend to the publication of rubrics and exemplars as well as information about the conditions under which the assessment occurred — time, resources available to students, and provisions for special-needs students.

4. Large-scale assessments should specify parameters — those mandated outcomes which are included in the assessment, and those which are not.

5. Large-scale assessments should provide teachers with specific information about how students performed on each of the identified outcomes.

These principles are especially critical for large-scale assessment mandated by school jurisdictions, provinces, and states. To the extent that the principles are respected, instruction of students will benefit; to the extent that they are ignored, instruction will be harmed. Through professional organizations, language arts teachers should advocate such principles. Large-scale performance assessments can benefit student learning when they emphasize the development of appropriate rubrics and the publication of related exemplars.

PROFESSIONAL DEVELOPMENT FOCUS:
Sharing an Understanding of Standards

• Participate in a group-marking session in which teachers employ a rubric to assess selected performances, e.g., writing samples, videotaped readers' theatre, and videotaped debates. Use differences in opinion as an opportunity to refine the rubric and to develop a shared understanding of standards. Consider whether the work samples are suitable as exemplars.

Ownership Issues in the Use of Exemplars

In recognizing the instructional potency of exemplars, teachers must always acknowledge student ownership of writing as well as of other language performances. No exemplar should ever be presented without the student owner's permission. Furthermore, teachers should do their best to ensure that students' work is honored when used for instructional purposes. They can do so by encouraging students to recognize desirable features and to offer constructive suggestions about the work.

Imagine the potential bombshell if a student or the child's parent objected to the sharing of a child's work — especially if the exemplar has sensitive content or if it represents less than perfect work. Just as in revision activities where students must decide whether or not to accept suggestions, students should have final say about presentations to public audiences.

For oral language, artistic, dramatic, and audiovisual presentations, students will recognize that a public audience is implicit. Language arts outcomes require students to make decisions about content, form and delivery appropriate for audience and purpose. No extraordinary permission is required for such formal performances since they are part of curriculum expectations. However, if teachers decide to keep a work sample or to preserve it on audiotape or videotape for future instructional use, they should seek the student's permission. In many cases, and also for writing exemplars, they would be wise to seek the parents' permission as well.

Students should learn that much of their writing completed for curriculum requirements, especially exploratory writing and early drafting, is inappropriate for public presentation. Sometimes, students will choose to share writing with teachers in confidence. The instructional relationship implies the teacher as audience. However, teachers should always seek the student's permission before they read aloud, post, publish or keep student writing as an exemplar. While response from audiences beyond the teacher is critically important for student writers, students should decide when to seek such response. After all, they own their writing.

Teachers are wise to use a letter form such as that on the next page when they collect exemplars.

Dear _____:

Please sign the attached permission slip so that I may employ the enclosed work sample written by your child as an instructional resource with other classes. Such samples are useful in instructing students about important curriculum expectations.

Please be assured that your child's work will be presented anonymously and that it will be honored as an instructional resource.

If you have questions or concerns, you can call me at _____.

Sincerely,

Anonymity makes sense with exemplars in that their instructional value is in the content rather than in the source.

PROFESSIONAL DEVELOPMENT FOCUS:

Respecting Student Ownership of Work

• Review school board or district policy on the collection and instructional use of student work

• With colleagues, develop a brief statement recognizing that permission should be sought when collecting exemplars.

An outcomes perspective clearly presents a range of challenges to language acts teachers: to balance assessment with an accent on performance assessment, to emphasize formative assessment of learning, to report student progress related to program modification, to encourage student self-assessment, to engage in group-assessment activities with colleagues, to develop rubrics, to collect exemplars, and to employ these exemplars as instructional resources. Since attention to these assessment challenges improves student learning, language arts teachers will certainly work on them collegially over the next several years. While it is true that teachers assess what they value, it is also true that most language arts teachers view improved student learning as the primary value of assessment.

CHAPTER FOUR

Coordinating and Communicating Critical Features of the Language Arts Program

Program Assessment by Teachers as Colleagues

In their reluctance to mandate methodology, outcomes curricula challenge individual teachers and their colleagues to make choices. Individually, teachers are always wise to offer a specific and rational account of their practice to students and parents. Collegially, teachers are wise to identify critical program features, approaches or methodologies which they are emphasizing throughout the grades. Students and parents benefit when they know what instructional approaches teachers emphasize and why teachers prefer certain approaches toward student achievement of outcomes.

This chapter presents a checklist of instructional features that have been clearly linked to student achievement of outcomes and documented in professional literature over several years. The list strives to show, rather than to tell what students and teachers are doing in effective language arts programs.

The checklist may be employed by individual teachers and colleagues toward program coordination and communication. Individual teachers may use it to reflect on the language arts programs in their own classrooms. Such reflection usually leads teachers to confirm many instructional practices and may possibly challenge them to set professional goals. Many school districts have adopted formative evaluation programs for teachers; in these districts, a checklist such as the following will align with growth-oriented and goal-directed teacher evaluation.

Individual teachers may use the checklist to foster their thinking about three critical questions:

1. What are the strengths and the growth areas for my language arts program?

2. What am I interested in learning and implementing so that I will grow professionally and will help students reach language arts outcomes/expectations more effectively?

3. How will I gather evidence to indicate the benefits of my program modifications?

Groups of teachers may complete the checklist as the first step in a discussion about the coordination and communication of the language arts program. However, the exercise is risky in that professional sensitivities are involved. In the light of curriculum outcomes and expectations, be sure to focus on the needs and interests of the school's students. What coordinated program features would *most* benefit students' language learning at this time? Avoid naming individual teachers throughout the resulting discussion.

Administrators can employ the following pages for program review and should do so collegially. Completing the assessment with teachers rather than about them is always wise. Ideally, administrators and teachers will work together to select program features for coordination and share perceptions of strength and need honestly and constructively.

Once a group of colleagues have completed the checklist individually, they can discuss

• program features that they perceive as strengths in the school
• program features that they perceive as needs appropriate for coordination across the grades

The group should choose no more than a few program features for coordination. Otherwise, their planning and implementation will lose focus. Remember that individual teachers may select their own goals to complement the goal setting done with colleagues.

LANGUAGE ARTS PROGRAM COORDINATION CHECKLIST

I. HOW OUR SCHOOL HELPS STUDENTS MEET OUTCOMES / EXPECTATIONS RELATED TO READING

PROGRAM FEATURES	PROGRAM STRENGTH	PROGRAM NEED
• Students sometimes read during class time and are encouraged to read at home.	————	————
• Students participate in pre-reading activities, including building background knowledge.	————	————
• Students are frequently encouraged to apply reading strategies. These include questioning, predicting, visualizing, considering familiar examples, and monitoring for understanding.	————	————
• Students are frequently encouraged to reconsider their interpretation of text based on careful rereading and on discussion.	————	————
• Students frequently talk about and write about connections between their new reading and past reading and between their new reading and personal experience.	————	————
• Students experience a balanced reading program which includes free-reading and guided reading.	————	————
• Students are encouraged to employ textual evidence to support interpretations and judgments.	————	————
• Students regularly read a variety of complete texts in different genres.	————	————

LANGUAGE ARTS PROGRAM COORDINATION CHECKLIST (*continued*)

II. HOW OUR SCHOOL HELPS STUDENTS MEET OUTCOMES / EXPECTATIONS RELATED TO WRITING

PROGRAM FEATURES	PROGRAM STRENGTH	PROGRAM NEED
• Students write for a variety of purposes and audiences and in a variety of forms.	————	————
• Students engage in appropriate pre-writing activities, such as interviewing, webbing, dramatizing, and diagramming.	————	————
• Students frequently engage in revision activities with an emphasis on applying appropriate specific criteria to revise writing.	————	————
• Students frequently present final draft writing to audiences.	————	————
• Students receive both praise and focused specific suggestions to improve their writing.	————	————
• Students participate in direct instruction related to work-in-progress.	————	————

III. HOW OUR SCHOOL HELPS STUDENTS MEET OUTCOMES / EXPECTATIONS RELATED TO ORAL LANGUAGE AND VISUAL COMMUNICATION

PROGRAM FEATURES	PROGRAM STRENGTH	PROGRAM NEED
• Students receive specific instructions, feedback, and modeling related to effective small-group participation.	————	————
• Students work in small groups with work-in-progress.	————	————

LANGUAGE ARTS PROGRAM COORDINATION
CHECKLIST (*continued*)

PROGRAM FEATURES	PROGRAM STRENGTH	PROGRAM NEED
• Students and teachers assess the effectiveness of small-group participation.	_____	_____
• Teachers employ small groups for focused instruction.	_____	_____
• Students and teachers perform and listen to oral reading (e.g., chants, plays, readers' theatre, oral interpretation of literature.)	_____	_____
• Students frequently present to audiences of peers and others.	_____	_____
• Students frequently work to solve problems, take risks and make independent decisions about their work-in-progress.	_____	_____
• Students frequently confer with teachers and other students about their work-in-progress.	_____	_____
• Students are encouraged to employ specific evidence to support positions and interpretations.	_____	_____
• Students are encouraged to analyse a variety of media messages, including combinations of word and image.	_____	_____
• Students are encouraged to create a variety of media messages.	_____	_____
• Students develop and employ appropriate criteria to assess publications, advertisements, films, graphics, and cartoons.	_____	_____

LANGUAGE ARTS PROGRAM COORDINATION
CHECKLIST (*continued*)

IV. HOW OUR SCHOOL HELPS STUDENTS MEET OUTCOMES / EXPECTATIONS THROUGH INSTRUCTIONAL PLANNING

PROGRAM FEATURES	PROGRAM STRENGTH	PROGRAM NEED
• Brief long-range plans outline approximate timelines, planned themes or topics, major expectations, principal resources, instructional procedures, and assessment techniques.	————	————
• Short-range plans are kept for current work-in-progress; these account for timelines, theme or topic, major learner expectations, specific resources, instructional procedures, and evaluation techniques. Short-range plans briefly include program modification notes.	————	————
• In most units, plans allow for student choice as well as for program modifications for individual students.	————	————
• Planning indicates the connection of content and strategies learned in different subjects, earlier in the term, or in a previous school year.	————	————
• Teachers employ students' work-in-progress to complete short-range planning.	————	————
• Students' learning of skills is always applied and connected to their current reading, writing, listening, speaking, or viewing activities.	————	————
• Planning indicates a commitment for teachers' modeling of strategies and to the presentation of exemplars to students.	————	————

LANGUAGE ARTS PROGRAM COORDINATION CHECKLIST (*continued*)

PROGRAM FEATURES	PROGRAM STRENGTH	PROGRAM NEED
• Planning indicates a commitment to the use of a variety of human, print, and media resources by individual learners.	_____	_____

V. HOW OUR SCHOOL HELPS STUDENTS MEET OUTCOMES / EXPECTATIONS THROUGH A PRODUCTIVE CLASSROOM ENVIRONMENT

• The classroom environment is supportive, with frequent acknowledgment and encouragement of all students.	_____	_____
• Students are frequently encouraged to value personal knowledge, to solve problems, to take risks, and to make independent decisions about their work-in-progress.	_____	_____
• Students frequently confer with teachers and other students about their work.	_____	_____
• Students work in varied grouping patterns — full class, small group and individual learning.	_____	_____
• Students have opportunities to investigate issues, to ask questions, and to present their findings to audiences.	_____	_____
• Students sometimes engage in modified learning activities.	_____	_____
• Students are offered a measure of choice in reading and writing content and in projects.	_____	_____

LANGUAGE ARTS PROGRAM COORDINATION CHECKLIST (*continued*)

VI. HOW OUR SCHOOL HELPS STUDENTS MEET OUTCOMES / EXPECTATIONS THROUGH ASSESSMENT

PROGRAM FEATURES	PROGRAM STRENGTH	PROGRAM NEED
• Students are challenged to employ specific criteria, to set personal learning goals, and to engage in self-assessment.	————	————
• Student progress is assessed through a variety of methods: checklists, observations, conferences, dated writing samples, and tests.	————	————
• Language arts assessment emphasizes performance assessment, but includes pre-specified response and observational assessment.	————	————
• Assessment of student learning is aligned to all expectations or outcomes.	————	————
• Assessment of student learning includes assessment of group performances or small-group work.	————	————
• Assessment of student learning includes specific feedback and encouragement for the learner.	————	————
• Students and teachers employ rubrics and exemplars for instruction and assessment.	————	————
• Reporting practice clearly informs parents about any modified expectations for their children.	————	————
• Standardized assessment is aligned with expectations in the prescribed language arts program.	————	————

Teachers and administrators need to communicate coordinated program features to parents as often as possible. They can do this through meetings and conferences with parents, as well as in publications. Students, parents, and community members should be challenged to assist the school's coordinated effort to help students reach outcomes more effectively. Such communication should highlight specific program features. Labels such as "process approach" and "whole language approach" are too general and often too emotionally charged to be helpful.

Throughout the program review, teachers and administrators may require professional development related to interpretation of program assessment criteria, as well as program development related to the coordinated implementation of selected program features. At the beginning of any program assessment, educators would benefit from reviewing proposed assessment criteria, such as those presented above in "Language Arts Program Coordination Checklist," to add, delete, and refine criteria. Such a review fosters ownership in the program coordination project. "Suggested Sequence for Groups to Complete a Review of Language Arts Program Coordination," on page 84, summarizes the steps educators could take to fulfil their program review.

Reconsidering Professional Development

The program coordination activities described in this chapter do not require an outcomes emphasis in education for implementation. However, an outcomes perspective certainly nudges educators toward program coordination and communication.

It is also clear that an outcomes perspective nudges educators to reconsider professional development. For years, teachers and administrators have viewed professional development as a personal matter. Educators have individually chosen to join professional organizations and to subscribe to publications of personal interest. Conventions, conferences, and in-service offerings typically take a menu approach; teachers select from a range of options. Without doubt, these wide-ranging activities continue to provide vital help to individual teachers to grow professionally according to personal needs and interests.

SUGGESTED SEQUENCE FOR GROUPS TO COMPLETE A REVIEW OF LANGUAGE ARTS PROGRAM COORDINATION

1. Teachers and possibly administrators could review and modify the assessment checklist as well as review the purpose of the exercise, to shortlist no more than three features for program coordination.

2. Teachers and administrators could individually complete the checklist to reflect on language arts program strengths and needs in the school, *not* in individual classrooms.

3. Teachers and administrators could meet to discuss their perceptions. They could begin by describing program strengths and then program needs — *not* program weaknesses.

4. Teachers and administrators could select one or two program features for coordination in the school.

5. Teachers and administrators could determine professional development, including publications and in-service sessions, which will help them to achieve their goals as well as to assess progress toward the goals.

6. Teachers and administrators could plan to communicate/ publicize their instructional focus for coordinated language arts and to invite students and parents to assist. Teachers and administrators could regularly assign meeting time to discuss successes and challenges in working together toward the selected goals.

7. Teachers and administrators could assess how well they are achieving program coordination goals on an ongoing basis.

Without denying the value of personal professional development, educators are increasingly recognizing the social and collegial dimension of professional development. For instructional programs to have coherence, educators must view professional development as shared learning required to complement personal learning. An outcomes perspective amplifies the question "What program features will we implement across the grades so that students meet outcomes more effectively?"

If educators agree that critical program features should be aligned, they might usefully consider taking part in professional development activities with their colleagues. Instead of *always* viewing professional development as a matter of individual choice, educators should make opportunities for teachers to reflect, to align practice and to plan cooperatively. Professional development should not always mean listening to a speaker or reading an article alone. An outcomes perspective challenges teachers and principals to confront the question "How much time do we allot for program coordination and communication in our school?" Staffs that do not plan systematically for collegial professional development will help students achieve outcomes less effectively than staffs that do.

PROFESSIONAL DEVELOPMENT FOCUS:
Planning Program Coordination

- Modify this chapter's program coordination checklist for use in your classroom or school.
- Make a plan for language arts program coordination for a group of teachers in your school. Consider helpful forms of collegial professional development.

CHAPTER FIVE

An Implementation Strategy for Any Newly Revised Language Arts Curriculum

How to Understand the Curriculum Document

Most language arts teachers would agree that legal curriculum documents are hardly bedtime reading. Some teachers might be tempted to remark that they require toothpicks to keep their eyes open during such reading.

Teachers themselves often require reading strategies to focus their attention on curriculum documents. While most Canadian language arts teachers have recently been challenged to implement revised curricula influenced by an outcomes perspective, teachers anywhere might usefully apply the following advice to make sense of any newly mandated language arts program document.

1. As you read, place a check (✔) beside any terminology or jargon which is new to you. For example, in the 1996 Western Protocol, at least some teachers will wonder about "media text" and "representing" as they read the Introduction. Does the document offer assistance in interpreting terminology — a glossary or footnote? Language arts teachers know that understandings of terminology vary; therefore, they are wise to check sources and to discuss interpretations.

2. Before reading the inevitable Introduction, take a minute to consider what you would write had you been its author. You would probably say something about how the expectations will be organized in the document, what is new and different,

and what statements of belief or philosophy about how language is learned apply. What would you predict for these sections? After your reading, consider which predictions were accurate. Identify at least one unexpected or surprising point about the following:

a) the organization of expectations or outcomes;
b) statements about new emphases in the program;
c) a belief about how children learn language.

3. Follow a similar process to review the expectations for the grade or for one of the grades that you teach. For each section or chunk of the curriculum document, examine the heading and predict what you will find in the section. Headings will vary. For instance, one outcomes-based document uses "Writing," "Reading," and "Oral and Visual Communication." Another, which refers to such headings as General Outcomes, provides more integrative headings. For example: "Explore thoughts, feelings, ideas and experiences," "Comprehend and respond personally and critically to literary and media texts" and "Enhance the clarity and artistry of communication." Once again, after your reading, consider which predictions were accurate. Identify at least one unexpected or surprising point in the category.

4. Examine the expectations or outcomes for the previous and subsequent grade to that which you have selected. Note and, if possible, discuss major differences. Which differences are most clearly expressed? Although exploring how expectations change over several grades might interest you, first focus on the grade you teach and surrounding grades to avoid bogging down in your reading and analysis.

5. Since educational research indicates that teachers first consider personal concerns and challenges whenever they implement a new curriculum, note and, if possible, discuss your major concerns with colleagues.

a) What are your major personal challenges in implementing this mandated program?
b) What are you being asked to add to, delete from and modify in your current language arts program?
c) How adequate are your current instructional resources?

d) What forms of assessment are required for the revised program?

e) What professional development — reading, videotapes, in-service — would be helpful?

Ideally, you can discuss these questions with colleagues, work with adequate instructional resources, and enjoy access to professional development. Indeed, *any* successful implementation of curriculum, whether it has an outcomes and standards emphasis or not, demands collegial exploration and coordination, adequate instructional resources, and relevant and regular professional development for teachers.

6. Analyse the wider context of the curriculum implementation. Note and, if possible, discuss critical factors which are not included in the legal document:
   a) standardized assessment practices in your school, jurisdiction or province;
   b) current political and media pressures;
   c) level of community and jurisdictional support available at your school;
   d) other current realities.

7. With colleagues, identify a few powerful program features which your school will coordinate to help students reach outcomes or expectations. Discuss how you will let students, parents and the community know about these features.

At its best, curriculum implementation affords educators the opportunity for personal reflection as well as collegial coordination. Such is true of all revised language arts curricula — with or without a standards and outcomes emphasis. The current emphasis on outcomes and standards encourages best practice to the extent that it fosters teachers' personal reflection and collegial coordination.

Aligning Curriculum with School Needs

Imagine the benefits to students when teachers across the grades commit themselves to aligning critical program features. Here is one such declaration of intent:

In our school, we will work together to help students develop their abilities as readers and writers. This year we are coordinating our efforts so that the following language arts program features are evident across the grades:

- We will encourage students to read intensively to determine meaning independently and to employ accurate and specific textual references to support their interpretations.

- Students will employ specific criteria to revise all writing taken to final draft.

From a standards and outcomes perspective, such a declaration is particularly relevant: each of the identified program features will enhance student learning and achievement. These general features relate directly to numerous specific reading and writing outcomes in curriculum documents. The declaration's wording fosters clear communication to students and parents. Furthermore, the declaration implies wide-ranging multidisciplinary and life skills applications.

The two identified program features will bear the most fruit if they become a coordinated focus in unit plans across the grades throughout the school year — the focus applies to *all* students, including those in modified programs. The two features imply balanced, formative, and performance assessments, as well as student self-assessment related to rubrics and exemplars. Although powerful, they are but alternatives among many program features that teachers might deem the most important for coordination in a given year.

Recommended References

Aker, Don. *Hitting the Mark: Assessment Tools for Teaching*. Markham, ON: Pembroke Publishers, 1995.

Alberta Education. *Classroom Assessment Materials Program*. Edmonton, AB: Education Advantage Inc., 1997.

Anderson, Richard, et al. *Becoming a Nation of Readers*. Washington, DC: National Institute of Education, 1985.

Applebee, Arthur. *The Child's Concept of Story*. Chicago, IL: University of Chicago Press, 1978.

Britton, James. *Language and Learning*. Harmondsworth, Eng.: Penguin, 1972.

Cunningham, Patricia, and R. L. Allington. *Classrooms That Work: They All Can Read and Write*. New York, NY: Harper and Collins, 1994.

Foster, Graham, Judy MacKay, and Claudette Miller. *Skills Instruction in a Language Arts Program*. Markham, ON: Pembroke Publishers, 1992.

Foster, Graham. *Student Self-Assessment: A Powerful Process for Helping Students Revise Their Writing*. Markham, ON: Pembroke Publishers, 1996.

Gollub, Jeff. *Focus on Collaborative Learning*. Urbana, IL: National Council of Teachers of English, 1988.

Graham, Neil, and Jerry George. *Marking Success*. Markham, ON: Pembroke Publishers, 1992.

Hillocks, George Jr. *Research on Written Composition, New Directions for Teaching*. Urbana, IL: National Council of Teachers of English, 1986.

Hillocks, George Jr. *Teaching Writing as Reflective Practice*. New York, NY: Teachers College Press, 1995.

Hydrik, Janie. *Parent's Guide to Literacy for the 21st Century*. Urbana, IL: National Council of Teachers of English, 1996.

Johnson, David W., et al. *Cooperative Learning in the Classroom*. Alexandra, VA: A.S.C.D. Publications, 1994.

McTeague, Frank. *Shared Reading in the Middle and High School Years*. Markham, ON: Pembroke Publishers, 1992.

Moffett, James, and Betty Jane Wagner. *Student-Centered Language Arts and Reading K–13*. New York, NY: Houghton Mifflin, 1976.

Monahan, Joy, and Bess Hinson. *New Directions in Reading Instruction*. Newark, DE: International Reading Association, 1988.

NCTE Staff. *Standards Consensus Series*. Urbana, IL: National Council of Teachers of English, 1997.

Oglan, Gerald, ed. *Writing Sense: Your Writing Skills Handbook*, Books 4, 5, and 6. Toronto: Harcourt Brace and Company Canada, 1996 and 1997.

Scraba, Elana. *Approaches to Writing by Grade 12 Students* (monograph). Edmonton, AB: Alberta Education, 1990.

Weaver, Constance. *Grammar for Teachers, Perspectives and Definitions*. Urbana, IL: National Council of Teachers of English, 1979.

Weaver, Constance. *Teaching Grammar in Context*. Portsmouth, NH: Heinemann, 1996.

Wing Jan, Lesley. *Spelling and Grammar in a Whole Language Classroom*. Brisbane, Aus.: Ashton Scholastic Ltd., 1991.

Index